IRONMAN'S
ULTIMATE GUIDE TO BUILDING
MUSCLE MASS

IRONMAN MAGAZINE AND PETER SISCO

CB
CONTEMPORARY BOOKS

Library of Congress Cataloging-in-Publication Data

Ironman's ultimate guide to building muscle mass / Ironman magazine
  and Peter Sisco [editor].
        p.   cm. — (Ironman series; bk.2)
      Includes index.
      ISBN 0-8092-2813-0
      1. Bodybuilding.   2. Muscle strength.   I. Sisco, Peter.
  II. Iron man.   III. Title: Ironman's ultimate guide to building
  muscle mass.   IV. Series.
  GV546.5.I773   1999
  646.7'5—dc21   99-23269
                                                            CIP

Cover design by Todd Petersen
Cover photograph by Michael Neveux
Cover model: Craig Titus
Interior design by Hespenheide Design

Published by Contemporary Books
A division of NTC/Contemporary Publishing Group, Inc.
4255 West Touhy Avenue, Lincolnwood (Chicago), Illinois 60712-1975 U.S.A.
Copyright © 2000 by *Ironman* magazine and Power Factor Publishing, Inc.
Printed in the United States of America
International Standard Book Number: 0-8092-2813-0

00 01 02 03 04 05 VL 18 17 16 15 14 13 12 11 10 9 8 7 6 5 4 3 2 1

Also in the *Ironman* series:

Ironman's Ultimate Bodybuilding Encyclopedia

CONTENTS

FOREWORD

Ironman magazine was founded in 1936 by Peary and Mabel Rader of Alliance, Nebraska. Their first print run of 50 copies was done via a duplicating machine that sat on their dining room table. *Ironman* started out as an educational vehicle to inform and enlighten those people who were interested in weight lifting, bodybuilding, and, eventually, powerlifting.

The focus of *Ironman* magazine during its first 50 years was on all three sports, with emphasis on weight training in general as a life-enhancing activity. *Ironman* has always stressed the health and character-building aspects of weight training and has always been the leader in bringing exercise and nutrition concepts and ideas to those in the training world.

In the early '50s, *Ironman* magazine was the first weight-training publication to show women working out with weights as part of their overall fitness regimen. It even went so far as to show a pregnant woman training with weights and educating readers on the benefits of exercise during pregnancy—thoroughly modern concepts 25 years ahead of its time. In the late '50s and early '60s, *Ironman* magazine was the first to talk about high-quality proteins derived from milk and eggs as well as liquid amino acids. The bimonthly magazine had, by this time, acquired over 30,000 subscribers simply on the strength of its information. The Raders never worked at expanding its circulation. It grew by word of mouth fueled by the general hunger for and *Ironman*'s ability to provide intelligent, timely, and reliable training information.

By the early '80s, the Raders, now in their 70s, had spent nearly 50 years working incredibly long hours to put out a bimonthly publication. The hard work was beginning to take its toll.

I'd been interested in *Ironman* as a business since the mid-'70s and had in fact talked several times with the Raders about purchasing *Ironman*. Eventually, my dream of owning and publishing a bodybuilding magazine was realized, and in August 1986, after 50 years, *Ironman* magazine changed owners. At that time, *Ironman* had a circulation of 30,000 subscribers, no foreign editions, was published bimonthly, and averaged 96 black-and-white pages except for a color cover. Thirteen years later, *Ironman* magazine is published worldwide with an English-language circulation of 225,000 and additional editions in Japanese, Italian, German, Arabic, and Russian.

The books in the *Ironman* series represent the "best of the best" articles from over 60 years of *Ironman* magazine. *Ironman's Ultimate Guide to Building Muscle Mass*, the second in this series, covers every aspect of bodybuilding physiology, targeting specific bodyparts, training for mass, optimum nutrition, avoiding injuries, and the hard-to-find tricks and secrets from the top champions.

John Balik
Publisher, Ironman

ACKNOWLEDGMENTS

I would like to thank the following people who made this book possible:

John Balik, publisher of *Ironman* magazine, had the foresight to see the need for this book and the others in the *Ironman* series. His knowledge of bodybuilding and his sensitivity to the information required by readers has made *Ironman* the best bodybuilding magazine in the world.

Steve Holman, editor in chief of *Ironman*, creates one informative, insightful issue of the magazine after another, and his own articles in this book show ample evidence of his innovation and encyclopedic knowledge of the iron game.

Mike Neveux is the premier bodybuilding photographer in the world. His photos in this book and in every issue of *Ironman* magazine have inspired and motivated countless bodybuilders around the world by capturing the intensity, power, and magnificence of these great athletes.

A special thanks to Terry Bratcher, art director of *Ironman*, who did an enormous amount of work in the preparation of this book by wading through *Ironman*'s immense archive of articles and photographs to help bring you the "best of the best."

Finally, I would like to thank all the writers who contributed to this book. These writers have an incalculable collective knowledge of the sport of bodybuilding. This book represents the distilled knowledge of hundreds of man-years of study in every aspect and nuance of the iron game. Between the covers of this book are wisdom and experience that would cost a small fortune to obtain from one-on-one training with these writers. Sadly, some are no longer with us to be able to share their vast insights, making their advice in these pages all the more valuable. It is the thought, effort, and writing of these individuals that make this book and *Ironman* magazine great.

Peter Sisco
Editor

INTRODUCTION

MASS—It's the indispensable element of bodybuilding. Mass is the marble from which all finely chiseled physiques must come. It's the reason we go into a gym and lift weights. Every time we lift a weight, whether we realize it or not, the purpose is to add mass somewhere on our body. At the very least, the purpose is to preserve the hard-won mass we have already developed.

Exercise science has conclusively proven that our bodies will only build more muscle mass when we push ourselves to the limits of our ability. But there are tricks and secrets that can make the road to ultimate muscularity and strength less prone to dead ends.

Ironman magazine has always been the front-runner when it comes to the science of training. For over 60 years it has chronicled the exercises and techniques that have proven themselves among the greatest bodybuilders of all time and among those just starting out in the sport. The information contained in this volume of the *Ironman* series will put you on the road to the fastest gains possible using tried and true techniques for adding maximum mass in minimum time.

Bodybuilding's legendary physiques such as those of Bill Pearl, Sergio Oliva, and Vince Gironda, combined with *Ironman*'s finest writers, including Steve Holman—one of the most knowledgeable people in the world on the subject of training—combine their hard-won experience and expertise to give you the answers you need for every phase of your training and development.

Study this book well, put the ideas into practice, and pack on MASS as you never have before.

Peter Sisco

Jean-Pierre Fux.

Chapter 1

POWER-MASS TRAINING
WORK HEAVY AND GET HUGE

BY GENE MOZÉE

Why can't you build impressive muscle mass and density? Is something stopping you from getting huge? Maybe you need a dose of power-mass training!

When I first began training many years ago, my goal was to get bigger so that I could play football and, of course, have a better physique. I gained 30 pounds in the first six months, and the additional muscle size and strength greatly enhanced my athletic ability. I became stuck, however, at 158 pounds and just couldn't gain another ounce no matter how hard I worked out or how many calories I consumed. I bounced around from gym to gym and tried every workout program used by bodybuilding champs such as Clancy Ross, Jack Delinger, and Reg Park. I was so confused that I was just about ready to throw in the towel and hang it up.

Fortunately, I met John Farbotnik at Muscle Beach in Santa Monica, California, and he invited me to his gym in Glendale. Farbotnik, who had won both the Mr. America and Mr. Universe titles in 1950, took my measurements and evaluated my physique and my training program. He explained to me that I was overtraining and overeating:

"To build greater muscle size and bodyweight, it takes proper activity, proper nutrition, and sufficient rest and sleep; to develop greater muscle mass, you need to use progressively heavier poundages and build greater power.

"Light warm-up exercises will never build the muscle size you want," Farbotnik emphasized.

"Light dumbbell movements like concentration curls, which are necessary for shaping and peaking the biceps, are fine, but who needs them to work on 15-inch arms? Hack squats are great for shaping the thighs, but if you want real muscle mass, you need heavy squats. You must handle consistently heavier weights in combination with a more scientific weight-gaining diet to reach your goals."

I soon found out that John knew his stuff. I joined his gym and gained 30 pounds in three months. My bench press went from 275 to 360. My arms went from $15^1/2$ inches to 18 inches, and my chest increased from 45 inches

There is no substitute for training heavy.

power or it doesn't react at all. There is no in-between, no compromise.

Your muscles are very economical, operating with as few fibers as they can. Light weights activate only a few muscle fibers, while heavy poundages stimulate the maximum number possible. As a muscle gets progressively stronger and larger, you must continually add more poundage to stimulate the maximum number of fibers. You have to constantly challenge your muscles to work harder and harder if you want to build dense, quality mass.

Unless you are a student of anatomy, you may be wondering what these deep-lying muscle fibers are. They are the auxiliary muscle fibers that attach to a major muscle group such as the biceps, pectorals, triceps, deltoids, or quadriceps and often surround its base. When they are bombarded with heavy power exercises, they thicken and increase in size, thus giving the muscle greater strength, more stamina, larger girth, improved shape, and increased fullness.

Generally speaking, performing an exercise with a moderate weight will produce only limited improvement. It will help shape and enlarge a particular muscle, but unless the deep-lying fibers of that muscle are aroused, it will never reach maximum development. Therefore, to activate those fibers and force your muscles to grow larger, you must blast them with the heaviest weapons in your arsenal—heavy power-mass exercises.

to 48 inches. At the same time, I found out that a substantial increase in body power produced a simultaneous increase in muscle mass.

BOMB THE DEEP-LYING FIBERS

The most effective way to produce greater muscle mass is to blast those deep-lying muscle fibers with heavy poundages. These submerged muscle fibers are rarely activated if you don't use heavy weights. A basic, scientific law, the all-or-none principle, operates in relation to muscle use: that is, an individual muscle fiber either reacts with all of its contractile

OVERALL GROWTH

When you attack the big, major muscle groups (chest, legs, back, and shoulders) with heavy power-mass exercises, all the other related muscle groups—primary, secondary, and tertiary—are stimulated into new growth. For example, when you do heavy bench presses in power-mass style, your deltoids, triceps, and even upper back receive extra benefits that make them larger and stronger and capable of handling heavier poundages on specific deltoid and arm exercises. This increased power is one of the keys to building the muscle mass and density you seek.

Anthony D'Arezzo.

POWER-MASS TRAINING PROGRAM

The following program was used by Marvin Eder, possibly the strongest bodybuilder who ever hoisted a barbell. In the '50s, Eder, along with George Eifferman, had the most massive pecs west of the Pecos. Eder was so strong that he bench-pressed 510 pounds and did standing presses with 365. He weighed 198, had 19-inch arms, and could do five sets of 10 reps with the 120-pound dumbbells in the seated press. He also did 12 one-arm chins with his right hand and 11 with his left. Eder told me that his secret to building record-breaking power and incredible muscularity was power-mass training. This exercise routine is the one he used, and it is the one he recommended to me. It not only helped me gain many pounds of muscle, but also pushed my bench press and overhead pressing strength to new heights.

Smith machine squats.

1. **Squats.** Keep the feet fairly close together. Elevate your heels on a $1\frac{1}{2}$- to 2-inch board. Squat to slightly below parallel to the floor, keeping your knees pointed forward. Inhale on the way down, and exhale when you come up.
2. **Bench presses.** Use a medium-wide grip, with your hands about 26 to 32 inches apart. Lower the bar slowly to the highest point on your chest while inhaling, and immediately ram it back to the top as you exhale.
3. **Heavy bent-over barbell rows.** Use the same hand spacing as for the bench press. Bend forward, with your back parallel to the floor, and pull the bar up until it touches your upper abdomen just below the bottom of the rib cage. Lower the bar slowly, close to your body, but don't let it touch the floor. Inhale on the way up, and exhale on the way down.
4. **Standing barbell presses.** Use a slightly wider-than-shoulder-width grip. Take the barbell off a squat rack rather than cleaning it, and preserve all of your energy for pressing. Wear a lifting belt to support your lower back. Exhale as

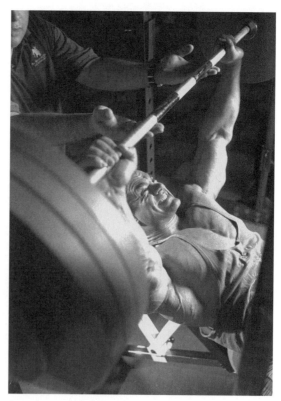

A spotter can help you lift safely.

you press the weight upward; inhale as you lower it. Do the reps rapidly, without pausing at the top or bottom.

5. **Lat machine pull-downs.** Using a fairly wide grip with your hands six to eight inches wider than shoulder width, pull the bar down to just below your collar bones until it touches your upper chest. Inhale during this pulling movement. Exhale as you slowly let the lats stretch as much as possible while you return the bar to the starting position. You can also substitute chins for this movement.

6. **Heavy dumbbell curls.** Do this exercise while seated on a sturdy bench. Use a slight cheating motion as you inhale, curling the dumbbells upward until they touch your delts. Exhale as you lower them all the way until your arms are straight.

7. **Cool down.** Do 100 leg raises.

TRAINING TIPS

- Train three times a week on alternate days.
- Perform each exercise for three sets of eight reps to start.
- After two weeks, increase to four sets of six reps.
- After 30 days, increase to five sets of six reps on each exercise.
- On the third month, increase to six sets of six reps.
- Relax and rest between each set and exercise, until you have recuperated enough to go on. This should be about two minutes.
- Schedule your workout so that you will have enough time to go through it completely without rushing.
- Don't add any other exercises.
- Don't engage in any strenuous sports or recreational activities while on this

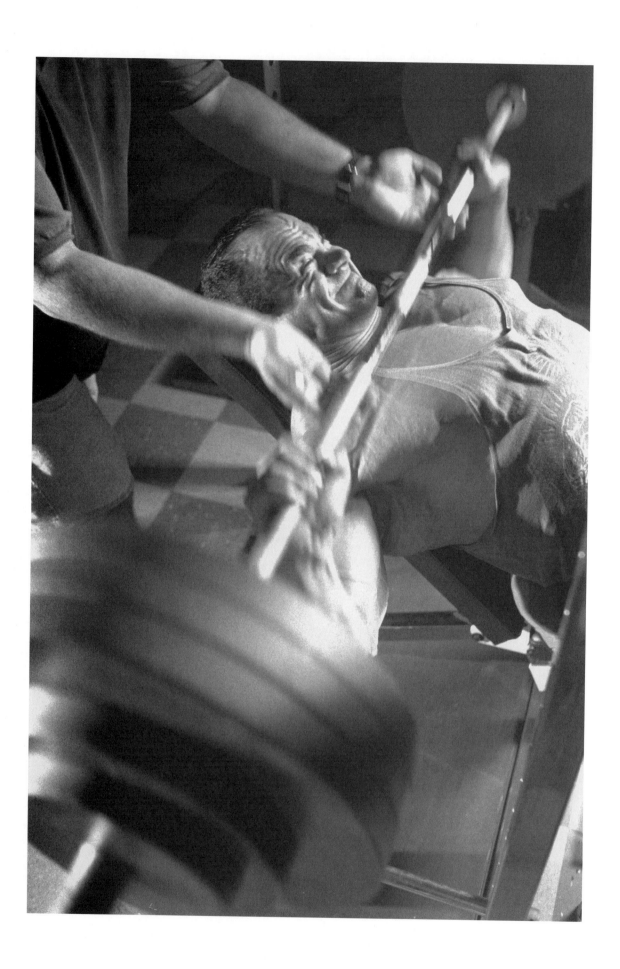

program. Save your energy for your workouts.

- Do one light warm-up set of 10 to 12 reps with a light weight—about 50 percent of your heaviest poundage—for each exercise. Then work up to as much weight as you can handle without straining.
- Follow the exercises in the order given.
- Stay with this program for at least three months without missing any workouts.
- Remember, to get maximum results, you need maximum effort. Increase the weight when you can do more reps than what is listed.

POWER-MASS NUTRITION

Get on a five-or-six-meal-per-day diet, eating a protein-rich meal or snack every three hours or so. Consume at least one gram of protein for every pound of bodyweight, plus an additional 10 percent for maximum growth. If you weigh 160, you need 160 grams of protein, plus an additional 20 to 25 grams (180 to 185 grams total). Eggs, milk, meat, fish, and poultry are the best sources of first-class muscle-building protein. To develop mass and make continuous weight gains, you need about 30 calories per pound of bodyweight every day, so stick to that if you want to gain 20 to 30 pounds of muscle in the next three months.

REST AND SLEEP

Eight to nine hours of sound, restful sleep *every* night is recommended. Also, never run when you can walk; never walk when you can stand still; never stand when you can sit; never sit when you can lie down; and when you do lie down, try to drift into a pleasant, growth-promoting sleep. Heavy power-mass training demands that you conserve energy outside of the gym whenever possible.

If you have been training regularly for at least six months and have gotten stale or reached a lack-of-progress plateau, try this power-mass training program to jolt your muscles into new growth. It has been used successfully by hundreds of bodybuilders and athletes. See what it can do for you.

Skip La Cour.

Chapter 2

MASS MACHINE TRAINING

BY SKIP LA COUR

Too many natural bodybuilders let short-term confusion throw them off course before they really begin their physique-building journey. "There are so many different training routines out there!" goes one common complaint. "How will I know for sure which routine or exercises will work for me? You know I can't train like those guys in the magazines who use steroids."

The uncertainty about whether their efforts will pay off often causes bodybuilders to make only a halfhearted attempt when they finally decide on a training regimen. Under those circumstances, what type of results can they really expect? If you give yourself the built-in excuse that a program won't necessarily work for you because you're natural, you aren't likely to be persistent when the gains don't come as quickly as you'd like.

Use sound judgment when choosing a training philosophy, but understand that you have to pick one and give it a try. Unfortunately, there's no guarantee that the first program—or the first dozen—will work best for you. You're not assured success in any-

thing in life. Things that are worthwhile don't come that easily. Success in bodybuilding works the same way. Don't have unreasonable expectations.

Every routine you try is a stepping-stone toward your ultimate success. If a routine doesn't work for you, don't curse the heavens; just move on to the next one. You've learned that something doesn't work for you, a valuable lesson that will serve you in the future— if you're persistent in your pursuit.

Have you ever been overwhelmed by a project, such as cleaning your garage? With so many different tasks involved, you had a difficult time deciding where to start, didn't you? When you finally stopped procrastinating and just attacked the project, those decisions became a lot easier. How about when you were a kid and you spent more time sitting at the edge of the pool, afraid that the water would be too cold, than you spent swimming?

Well, jump right in—the water's fine! Stop searching for guaranteed success, because it doesn't exist. As a bodybuilder, the more I learn, the less I really know. The challenge of

coming up with the right strategies to make your body grow is both fascinating and frustrating. The key to enjoying bodybuilding is to see your training as fascinating rather than frustrating. The choice is yours.

THE ANSWERS ARE OUT THERE

No matter what your questions are about training, the answers are waiting for you to find them. Maybe you'll find them in this chapter or in an issue of *Ironman*. Maybe there's a book or a website that contains some key information. Maybe that guy in your gym who isn't so muscular but is incredibly knowledgeable can help. I can't say where you'll find the answers, but I can tell you with certainty that they exist.

The question is, Will you be persistent enough to find them? Believing that the knowledge is there for you to find will empower you to maximize your training efficiency. You'll live in a state of anticipation that the next magazine, book, or conversation

will reveal the secrets that will finally bring you the muscular physique you've been working so hard to attain. You'll feel more in control of your bodybuilding destiny.

TAKE RESPONSIBILITY FOR SUCCESS AND FAILURE

Bodybuilding can be a very difficult endeavor, so be proud when you make significant gains. You deserve the rewards for your consistent effort. Your determination, knowledge, and implementation of good training techniques have produced results for you. Congratulations!

At the same time, take responsibility when your training isn't going quite as well as you'd like. Too many natural bodybuilders want to blame their poor results on the fact that they don't use drugs or that they have poor genetics. They're quick to find scapegoats and never put the responsibility squarely on their own shoulders. Many of the bodybuilders I talk with—whether they are young or old, have weeks of training experience or many years,

Many people refuse to accept that training each muscle group only once a week leads to significant muscle growth.

the gym? Are you constantly challenging yourself to take things to a higher level? Are you actively seeking new, improved methods to make your training more effective—or are you comfortable with the belief that you know almost everything you need to know?

I urge you to adopt immediately the empowering belief that there's always a higher level of development to shoot for. Never settle for less than what you really want out of your physique. It doesn't matter what you've accomplished in the past; you can always accomplish more. There's always one more pound of weight to lift, one more pound of muscle to add to your frame, or one more inch a certain bodypart can expand—if you're truly committed to doing it.

MAXIMUM INTENSITY IS ESSENTIAL

Training with maximum intensity is the cornerstone of an effective muscle-building program. The question is, How do you know if you're actually using max intensity?

Why is it you can instantly lift a lot more weight for more repetitions than ever before after seeing your rival in the gym do it? You didn't know you had it in you, did you?

Intensity means constantly putting the pressure on yourself to crank it up a notch on every set of every workout of every week. Maximum intensity—at least for me—means lifting extremely heavy weights with a goal-oriented, determined, and focused mind-set.

NEVER STOP STRIVING FOR MORE

have accomplished relatively little yet or are national champions—feel comfortable that they understand proper training methods. If they have problems, they usually blame them on their lack of drugs or their bad genetics. They never seriously reevaluate their training strategies.

Are you really doing everything you can to become your very best? How's your focus in

In terms of gauging maximum intensity, I've discovered some barometers that give me a pretty good idea. Have you ever noticed that the number of repetitions you can get on a specific exercise varies from workout to workout even though you're using the same weight? That says a lot about your training intensity. If you normally perform nine repetitions with a certain weight but sometimes can get only six,

Training with maximum intensity is the cornerstone of an
effective muscle-building program.

that shows a considerably lower intensity level. You suffer a 33 percent decrease in performance. Multiply that deficiency by a year's worth of workouts, and think about how much muscle you'll fail to gain—and how much frustration you'll feel.

It's awesome that you can get yourself into peak performance mode when your rival hits the gym, but why do you need someone else to drive you to perform so well? How much better would you be—and how much more muscle would you build—if you could generate the same intensity by yourself during the majority of your workouts?

EMOTION IS EVERYTHING

Try this experiment: Before attempting a set during your next workout, get yourself ready for maximum intensity by putting yourself in a peak emotional state of mind. Try to remember a specific time when you felt that you were especially strong and powerful. Do you remember how good that felt? Close your eyes, and experience that memory over and over again.

Open your eyes and do your set. If you've fully associated and stepped into that powerful experience from your past, you should immediately become more powerful. Emotion is everything when it comes to training with intensity.

HEAVY TRAINING IS THE SECRET

I firmly believe that heavy weight training can build significant drug-free mass. I realize that not everyone shares my view. "Bodybuilding is about working the muscle—not about how much weight you can lift!" How often have you read that in the magazines?

It's difficult to argue with people who use less weight and higher reps and are happy with their progress, but think of how much more muscle they'd have if they focused on lifting heavier weights.

The body is a great adapting machine. Hypertrophy, or growth, occurs when you heavily tax, or overload, the muscle. The body adapts by building muscle to prepare itself to lift that weight again in the future. In other words, if you build your biceps to 15 inches by lifting 50-pound dumbbells, you'll need to lift more than 50 pounds to push them to 16 inches.

If you understand that line of thought, then you may also agree that the muscle will stay the same size if you lift the same amount of weight. Obviously, if you lift lighter weights, the muscle will get smaller, or atrophy.

Which do you think will help you build more muscle mass: performing more reps or constantly challenging yourself to lift more weight? It's indeed possible for you to make tremendous gains in strength—especially if you break them down into bite-size pieces. Start by challenging yourself to lift just five pounds more. Once you build the confidence you need, try increasing your goal to 10 more

pounds, and so on. Get some help from a spotter if you need it, but try to lift heavier weights. A reliable training partner who's ready to grab the weight in case you fail will help you be more comfortable as you push yourself to lift bigger weights.

LESS VOLUME MEANS MORE MUSCLE

Since you're reading this publication, I assume that you're an ambitious bodybuilder who's willing to work very hard to reach your goals. Unfortunately, that attitude can sometimes be a hindrance when it comes to training efficiency.

When I first started training, I wanted to get big so badly, and I was more than willing to put forth the extra effort. Naturally, I believed that the secret to getting big was to train more often. How wrong I was.

Back then, I used a three-on/one-off training regimen—and rarely took the one day off. Through pure determination, I was able to muster some gains, but not because I was using the most efficient training method. With most things in life, the more you do them, the better you become. That, however, doesn't apply to bodybuilding and training—especially for natural athletes.

Recuperation is an important ingredient in muscle building. Overloading your muscles with heavy weights breaks them down. To grow most efficiently, your muscles must completely heal, or recover, before you train them again. Steroids help drug users' muscles recover more quickly and allow them to train again sooner. Training a muscle over and over in that optimal growth environment is what makes steroids so effective.

As a drug-free bodybuilder, you have no such advantage. You must wait for nature to restore the muscles' best environment for growth. Training before nature completes that job reduces training efficiency.

As a natural bodybuilder, how many times a week do you think you can effectively train a muscle? If I suggested you could do it 10 times a week, you'd find that absolutely ridiculous. What about five times a week? I imagine you're still shaking your head.

Most natural bodybuilders believe that they should work each muscle two times a week. I submit to you that the magic number is one—you should train each bodypart once a week, blasting it with the utmost intensity.

ONCE-A-WEEK-PER-BODYPART TRAINING

It was Paul Delia, the president of AST Sports Science, who suggested that I abandon my three-on/one-off training program and adopt the less-is-more philosophy. Switching to once-a-week-per-bodypart training launched me into an unbelievable course of new muscle growth.

My training benefited both physically and mentally. My size exploded as I became stronger and recovered much more efficiently.

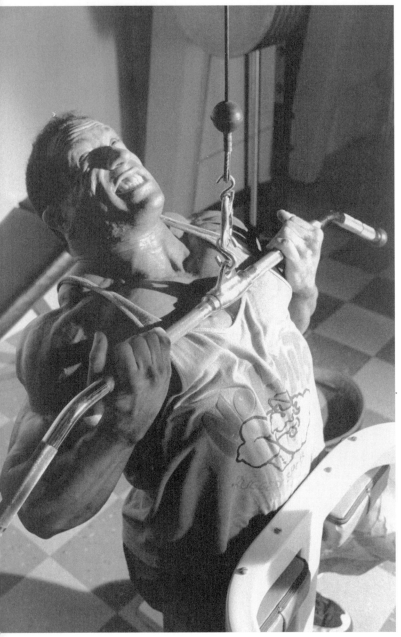

Dave Palumbo.

I developed the confidence to train heavier and heavier. By concentrating on only a single muscle group per day, I also became more focused. I created a do-or-die attitude at every training session, since I knew it was my only chance all week to stimulate that particular muscle group to grow. I had to train efficiently if I was going to build the body of my dreams.

There are many people who still believe that more must be better. They refuse to accept that training each muscle group only once a week leads to significant muscle growth. If not for the physical benefits, try the regimen beginning on page 44 for a couple of weeks for the mental boost. Even if you switch back to your old routine, I'll bet you'll find it very difficult to match that intensity level—it will become your new standard.

THE ONLY PURPOSE FOR A WARM-UP

Lighter, warm-up weights serve an important purpose: to prepare your muscles to attack safely the much heavier weights that stimulate growth. Many bodybuilders use warm-up weights for a few sets on the very first exercise for a particular bodypart. That's not only acceptable—it's essential. After you've sufficiently warmed up the muscle, however, you don't need to do any more light sets for it. Warm-up weights don't build muscles, so it's important that you don't waste your precious energy. On the exercises listed in the routine, go straight to the heaviest weight you can lift.

PICK THE RIGHT NUMBER OF EXERCISES

I believe that you don't need any more than two exercises—three at the most—to encourage muscle growth for most bodyparts. The secret is that you have to perform those exercises with the right level of intensity.

For larger bodyparts such as back and legs, I do a few more exercises; however, chest, biceps, triceps, shoulders, calves, and abdominals are simpler groups, and there are only

More strength and better recovery led to a lot of new muscle.

What was even more amazing was the way that the training regimen affected me mentally. Since I no longer needed to pace myself through long, grueling sessions, my workouts became more like sprints than marathons, and my training intensity, which I'd thought was pretty darn good, went through the roof.

so many ways you can hit them. Adding more exercises for them is just doing more of the same.

As for the number of sets, doing two per exercise has proven sufficient for me. When you're training only one bodypart per day, a thorough, efficient workout should take no longer than an hour.

HOW MANY REPS BUILD MUSCLE?

The real question is: How many repetitions does it take for you to start feeling the target muscle taxing itself? Twelve reps? Ten? Eight? Four? Two?

If you really don't start feeling the weight until the eighth rep, you should consider using heavier weight and feeling it earlier in the set. The heavier, the better, remember?

On my work sets, I aim for four to six repetitions. If I can do more than six, I know I've picked a weight that's too light. Conversely, if I can't properly perform four repetitions, the weight is too heavy. Either way, I make the proper adjustment, not only for the next set but also for every workout I'll do in the future.

PROPER FORM

There's no point in lifting extremely heavy weights if you use sloppy form. The trick is to become good on your form while using heavier weights. You do that by practicing.

Whether you want to hit a golf ball straight down the fairway, shoot a basketball through a hoop, or lift a heavy weight with good form, you need to practice. Don't shy away from attacking the heavier weights because your form isn't very good at the very beginning. Keep working at it.

Use a weight that's heavy enough to properly overload the muscle, even if your form isn't perfect. Strive to improve your form with the heavier load. I don't recommend sticking with extremely light weights just so that you can use perfect form.

Alternate dumbbell curls.

SYNERGY MAKES YOUR EFFORTS SUCCESSFUL

I know many bodybuilders who consistently train like animals in the gym but fail to get the results they deserve. What you do during that hour in the gym is very important, but what you do during the other 23 hours of the day may be even more important.

Synergy can be defined as the working together of many different factors to produce a single result. Your success as a bodybuilder will be determined not only by how well you train in the gym, but also by the synergy created by your training, nutrition, supplementation, and motivational strategies. To become the very best you can be, you must examine your habits in all of those areas.

SKIP LA COUR'S TRAINING SCHEDULE

Day 1: Chest
Day 2: Back
Day 3: Quadriceps
Day 4: Arms
Day 5: Shoulders
Day 6: Hamstrings
Day 7: Rest

Day 1: Chest

Flat-bench presses	
(warm-up)	5 × 10, 8, 6, 2, 2
(work sets)	2 × 4–6
Incline flyes	2 × 4–6
Incline dumbbell presses	2 × 4–6

Day 2: Back

Pull-ups (warm-up)	6 × 10–12
Dumbbell rows	2 × 4–6
Pull-overs	2 × 4–6
Lat pulldowns	2 × 4–6
Reverse-grip lat pulldowns	2 × 4–6
Cable rows	2 × 4–6

Day 3: Quadriceps

Leg extensions	
(warm-up)	4 × 12
(work sets)	2 × 4–6
Hack squats	2 × 4–6
Squats	
(warm-up)	2 × 10–12
(work sets)	2 × 4–6
Wide-stance leg presses	2 × 4–6
Lunges	2 × 4–6

Day 4: Arms
Biceps

Alternate dumbbell curls	
(warm-up)	2 × 12, 10
(work sets)	2 × 4–6
Barbell curls	2 × 4–6

Triceps

Dumbbell extensions	
(warm-up)	2 × 10–12
Cable pushdowns	2 × 4–6
Lying EZ-curl bar extensions*	2 × 4–6

*A.k.a. skull crushers.

Leg extensions, start.

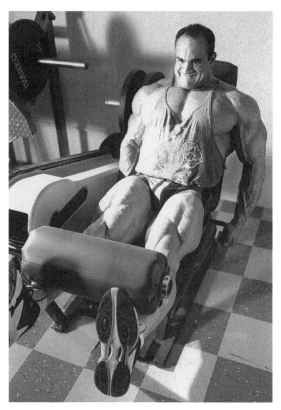

Leg extensions, finish.

Cable pushdowns.

Seated dumbbell presses, start.

Seated dumbbell presses, finish.

Forearms

Wrist curls	2 × 12
Reverse wrist curls	2 × 12

Day 5: Shoulders

Smith machine military presses	
(warm-up)	5 × 12, 10, 6, 2, 2
(work sets)	2 × 4–6
Lateral raises	2 × 4–6
Dumbbell presses	2 × 4–6
Bent-over lateral raises	2 × 4–6

Day 6: Hamstrings

One-leg leg curls	
(warm-up)	2 × 10–12
(work sets)	2 × 4–6
Stiff-legged deadlifts	2 × 4–6
Reverse hack squats	2 × 4–6
Reverse lunges	2 × 2–6

Day 7: Rest

SKIP LA COUR'S TOP 10 DRUG-FREE MASS-BUILDING TRAINING STRATEGIES

1. Train very heavy most of the time. The muscles must be constantly overloaded to continue growing. Repetitions should be in the four-to-six range.

2. Constantly challenge yourself to lift more weight. Never settle for less weight than you've done in the past.

3. After warming up a bodypart with the first exercise, don't waste the time or energy warming it up again on other movements. Go straight to the heaviest weight possible.

4. The form you use should be reasonably good for the weights you lift. If the weight is too heavy, your form will be too sloppy to be effective. If the weight is too light, you may be sacrificing progress for the sake of great form. Big weights make big muscles—period. Try to use the heaviest weight you can lift with decent form.

5. Perform every set to absolute failure; in other words, you can't do even one more rep.

6. Keep your exercises to a minimum: two or three on smaller muscle groups, five or six on the larger groups.

7. Get a lot of rest before training the muscle again. One bodypart a week, spread over six days, has proved ideal for me. Always take the seventh day off.

8. Back up your training with sound nutrition—especially with high-quality whey protein.

9. Enhance your training with good supplementation. Get all the information you can, and take advantage of the tremendous advances in that important area—but don't depend on supplements alone to create your physique. As the word implies, supplementation is something you use in addition to intense training and sound nutrition.

10. Be consistent. My training and diet seven months out from a show are just as important as they are seven weeks—or even seven days—out.

Mohamed Makkawy.

Chapter 3

RESURRECTION
TRIED-AND-TRUE WORKOUTS FOR MODERN-DAY MASS

BY C. S. SLOAN

In their ongoing quest for greater strength and more muscle, bodybuilders will try any new routine that comes their way. Every month, they scan the latest issues of the muscle magazines, hoping to find a routine or technique that will finally give them the physique they want. They'd be better off, however, if they took a look at the muscle-building techniques that have been around for years.

The best methods for getting bigger and stronger have never changed. What worked for John Grimek and Bill Pearl still works today.

Many trainees look at the size and condition of pro bodybuilders and think that because they're so much larger and more ripped than the old-time bodybuilders, they must know more about training. They conveniently forget what a large part androgenic steroids, which promote male characteristics, and other performance-enhancing drugs have played in building the pros' physiques. Nor do many of today's natural bodybuilders compare to yesteryear's lifters, despite more sophisticated use of nutrition and supplementation.

The key difference lies in the way bodybuilders used to train. Go into any gym and count the number of people using heavy deadlifts, squats, bent-over rows, bench presses, military presses, and straight-bar curls. I'll bet you half of my muscle that you'll see at least 75 percent of the people there screwing around with multiple exercises on machines and cables and isolation crap—you know, concentration curls, flyes, lateral raises.

If you want to get huge, not to mention incredibly strong, you owe it to yourself to try out some of these methods. Use any of the following routines for six weeks, and you're guaranteed new size and power.

THREE-DAYS-A-WEEK FULL-BODY BLAST

As recently as 15 years ago, people still believed in using whole-body workouts. If you were a beginner, you always used this kind of training schedule. Intermediate or advanced

Leg presses.

trainees who hit a rut always went back to it to get growing again. Use a Monday-Wednesday-Friday or Tuesday-Thursday-Saturday rotation. Trust me: if you do this program as described, you won't be tempted to train more frequently.

Workout 1

Squats	5 × 5*
Bench presses	5 × 5*
Chins	5 × 5*
Dips	5 × 10**
Dumbbell curls	5 × 10**

*Do two progressively heavier warm-up sets followed by three work sets. It should be really tough to do five reps on all three sets. Once you can get five reps on all three sets, add 10 to 20 pounds and start over the next time you use this workout.

**Do two progressively heavier warm-up sets of 10 reps followed by three work sets, using enough weight to make it damned hard to perform three sets of 10.

George Olesen.

Squats.

Workout 2

Deadlifts	5 × 5*
Standing military presses	5 × 5*
Barbell curls	5 × 5
Close-grip barbell presses	5 × 5

*Do two progressively heavier warm-up sets followed by three work sets with your top weight for five reps.

Workout 3

Squats	5–6 × 2*
Bench presses	5–6 × 2*
Hammer curls	5–6 × 2*
Flat-bench or incline dumbbell presses	5 × 5**
Stiff-legged deadlifts	5 × 5

*Do several progressively heavier warm-up sets of two reps until you reach the absolute maximum weight you can handle for two all-out reps. Do your final set at 90 percent of your one-rep max. If you're new to low-rep training, you may need to take it easy the first few times and use a weight that's 75 to 80 percent of your one-rep max. After that, don't hold back.

**Use the same format as the one listed for squats in Workout 1.

This program may be simple, but it's not easy, especially if you use appropriate poundages. If you do, you won't be able to train more than three times per week.

SINGLE-REP TORTURE

The idea of a workout composed entirely of single-rep training may go against everything you've been led to believe about building muscle. Heavy singles are dangerous; singles don't build muscle; singles are old-fashioned—I've heard it all. Fifty years ago, there were plenty of strongmen and lifters who built loads of muscle using heavy single-rep training. They didn't worry about "scientific" bodybuilding; they just tried things out and discovered what worked. That's what you need to do. Try the following program for at least four weeks. Train four days a week with a two-on/two-off rotation.

Stiff-legged deadlifts, start.

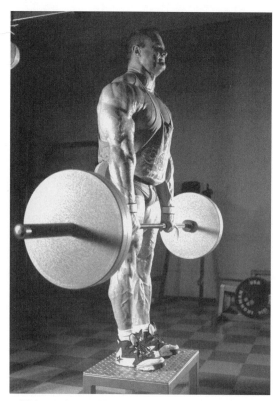

Stiff-legged deadlifts, finish.

Workout 1

Deadlifts	5–7 × 1
Partial-rep squats	4–5 × 1

Do several progressively heavier deadlifts until you work up to your top set with a weight that's 90 to 95 percent of your one-rep max. If your max is 500 pounds, your sets would be 135 × 1, 225 × 1, 315 × 1, 405 × 1, 455 × 1, and 475 × 1. Stick with your top weight for one to three singles, taking two to four minutes' rest between sets.

For the partial squats, set the pins in the power rack so that you squat to about a quarter of the way down. You should be significantly stronger on this exercise than on the full-range movement. If you max out at 405 on the regular squat, shoot for a top single of around 500 pounds. You won't need as many warm-ups after your deadlifts, so your sets might look something like this: 225 × 1, 315 × 1, 405 × 1, 495 × 1.

Workout 2

Bottom-position bench presses*	4–5 × 1
Weighted wide-grip chins	4–5 × 1
Incline presses	4–5 × 1
Standing military presses	4–5 × 1
Barbell curls	4–5 × 1

*Set the pins in the power rack so that you begin this exercise with the bar brushing your chest. That lets you do heavy singles safely while making the movement even tougher.

As in the first workout, do progressively heavier singles until you reach your top weight. You may want to alternate the bench presses with the chins in a slow superset fashion.

Workout 3

Squats*	5–7 × 1
Deadlifts**	4–5 × 1

*Use a full range of motion, making sure that you're thoroughly warmed up before handling your top weight.

**If you have access to heavy-enough dumbbells, do dumbbell deadlifts. Otherwise, do regular or power rack deadlifts.

Craig Titus.

The legendary Bill Pearl.

Workout 4

Floor presses*	4–5 × 1
Hammer curls	4–5 × 1
Close-grip bench presses**	4–5 × 1
Reverse barbell curls	4–5 × 1

*Lie down in the power rack, and set the pins so that you move the bar four to six inches. It's extremely difficult to cheat on this movement, which makes it very effective.

**Begin these in the bottom position of the power rack, just as you did for the regular bench presses in Workout 2.

These four single-rep workouts are all short and simple, but they're also extremely hard and effective. Each work set should be a battle to complete the one rep.

ADVANCED POWER RACK WORKOUT

Once you've been training for a while and built up your strength, it's almost a necessity to start using the power rack. It lets you really overload your muscles with heavy, heavy weights. You can use huge poundages safely while working alone, and you can use lockout movements on the basic compound exercises. All of the movements in this workout are performed in the power rack. It's a demanding routine, but you'll reap big gains if you're willing to tough it out. You hit each major bodypart once a week, following a three-days-a-week schedule. You'll need the rest, believe me.

Workout 1

Bottom-position incline presses*	5–7 × 1
Bottom-position close-grip bench presses	4–5 × 3**
Bench press lockouts***	5 × 5

*Get in the power rack with an incline bench, and set the pins so that the bar brushes against the top of your chest in the bottom position. Warm up with five or six progressively heavier singles until you reach an almost-maximum poundage for one rep.

**Do three or four progressively heavier triples until you reach the maximum weight you can handle for one or two sets of three reps.

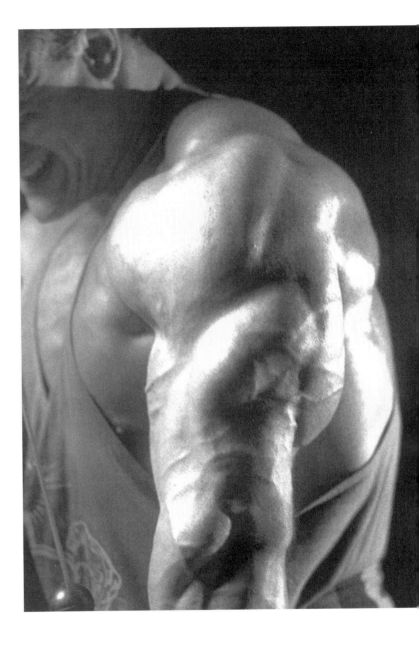

***Set the pins so that you move the bar through a range of motion that's close to lockout.

Workout 2

Bottom-position squats*	5 × 3
Squat lockouts**	4–5 × 1

*Set the pins so that you start your squat from the bottom position. This one's a killer, but it will really bring your strength up. Warm up over four progressively heavier triples to a maximum.

**Set the pins so that you're moving the weight with a range of motion that's less than a quarter squat.

Workout 3

Deadlifts from the knees	6–7 × 1
Standing ¼ military presses	4–5 × 3
Standing shrugs*	5 × 5
Barbell curls	4–5 × 1

Always ease into a power rack program, because it's demanding even for the advanced lifter. Don't rush it, or you may injure yourself.

*Set the pins a little below your waist so that you rest the bar briefly after each rep.

Jean-Pierre Fux.

ONE EXERCISE, MULTIPLE SETS

The following routine is composed of two sessions, so you can vary your schedule—two on/one off, two on/two off, every other day, or just every two to three days, whenever you feel you've recuperated.

Workout 1

Bench presses	6 × 6
Wide-grip chins	6 × 6
Standing military presses	6 × 6

For all of these movements, choose a weight that you can normally use for 10 reps. Do six straight sets with only a minute's rest between them. The first couple of sets won't be bad, but after that, you'll find this is a very tough workout.

Workout 2

Squats	5 × 15*
Close-grip bench presses	6 × 6**
Barbell curls	6 × 6

*Pick a weight with which you would normally be able to do 20 reps, and try for five sets of 15, with only a minute's rest between sets. Shoot for at least three sets your first workout, and work up to five.

**Follow the same approach as described for Workout 1.

These are very short workouts but extremely taxing. Once you can do the prescribed number of sets and reps, increase the weight by 10 to 15 percent the next time you do the workout, and start over.

There you have it—four intense, abbreviated routines using only basic compound movements that really pack on the mass and power. Don't worry about their being old-fashioned—they'll give you a real workout and real muscle.

Forcing blood into the muscle and inducing a pump causes
new capillaries to form in the target muscle, which increases
the muscle's size.

Chapter 4

THE MASS-BUILDING HARDGAINER SOLUTION

BY STEVE HOLMAN

Your metabolism races faster than a revving Testarosa, your wrists and ankles have the diameters of twigs from an undernourished sapling, and your muscle growth is about as fast as a snail on Quaaludes. In bodybuilding, you're known as a hardgainer, but a better description would be genetically cursed. You believe you have about as much chance of hitting poses in front of a cheering crowd as Howard Stern has of becoming president of the Daughters of the American Revolution—even if he does look mighty fetching in a skirt and panty hose. It's impossible for you to attain a competition-worthy physique, right? Not so fast, there, fellow hardgainer.

Allow me to revert to first person for a few paragraphs and regale you with my own story. It's important for you to know that I'm not some genetic Dorian Yates–type superfreak telling hardgainers how to train. That would be like Troy Aikman trying to teach a guy with no arms how to throw a football 50 yards.

I'm far from being gifted in the muscle-building department. Talk about genetically cursed! My father weighed all of 115 pounds—no doubt after a big meal—when he married my mother, who weighed a whopping 95, fully clothed and holding a large purse. It was a union of two string-bean physiques: Barney Fife meets Olive Oyl. At 16, I was the spitting image of my rail of a father in his teenage years—OK, so I had him by about 5 pounds; I weighed in at just under 120—and my most-muscular looked like newsreel footage from the World War II concentration camps.

When you're that skinny in high school, you do one of three things: you turn into an introvert and get beaten up a lot, join the chess club and get beaten up a lot, or lift weights so the thought of beating you up crosses fewer people's minds.

Of course, I was still damn skinny all through high school, even with my intense weight-training sessions. I was 5'10", and my bodyweight hovered around 160 during my senior year. I'm sure many readers can identify with that plight, but even at 160, I had enough visible muscle on my frame to ward off the majority of beatings. If bullies see a hint of sinew, they tend to look elsewhere for a victim.

Nevertheless, I was the living embodiment of Jolly Roger, the skull-and-crossbones figure on pirate flags, when I entered college, which may account for my voracious thirst for bodybuilding knowledge. I knew it held the key to overcoming my physical inadequacies—if only I could determine the perfect training routine that would pack mass on my bamboo-shoot body.

At the University of Texas at Austin, I hit the books hard, doing most of my research papers on muscle growth and the best way to trigger it. I combed the science libraries for hypertrophy-related studies and abstracts, and lo and behold, I actually uncovered a number of things that made efficient muscle building much easier, especially for hardgainers.

For example, I learned that the myotatic reflex occurs when a muscle is stretched and then forced to contract soon thereafter. The stretch puts the target muscle in an emergency-response mode, which can cause an inordinate number of muscle fibers to fire. In other words, you get more growth stimulation from each rep when the myotatic reflex is engaged. If you use it right, this technique can cause you to leapfrog genetic growth limitations by tricking the nervous system into believing it must grow in order to prevent severe trauma, as in muscle tears.

I took this knowledge into the gym and made some of the best gains of my life. My body weight eventually shot over the 200-pound mark, and I entered and won my very first bodybuilding contest. People were even accusing me of being an easy gainer.

This metabolic shift out of the genetic trash bin didn't just magically happen, however. It took a lot of experimentation. While it's true that, once I identified and began using a stretch-position movement for each bodypart, my gains increased significantly, I also had to go back to my research and hone the other factors that contribute to muscle growth.

Joe Spinello.

TRIGGERING HYPERTROPHY

According to Michael Wolf, Ph.D., the following changes are associated with increases in muscle size and strength:

1. The actin and myosin protein filaments increase in size.
2. The number of myofibrils increases.
3. The number of blood capillaries within the fiber may increase.
4. The amount of connective tissue within the muscle may increase.
5. The number of muscle fibers may increase.

If you train in the 7- to 12-rep range with heavy weights often enough, you stress the type-2, or fast-twitch, muscle fibers, which will positively affect the actin and myosin filaments and increase the number of myofibrils (1 and 2 on the preceding list). Most

the muscles will help you attain a skin-stretching pump in the shortest time possible. Remember, with your limited recovery ability, you can't waste time and energy doing endless sets to get a pump that increases the number of capillaries. You have to blow up the muscle in a few sets and then get out of the gym so you can grow.

Try to eat some carbohydrates at every meal, which means six times a day, along with your feedings of 30 to 40 grams of protein. Don't be afraid of taking in some fat at a few of your meals, either. New research says that fat can help bolster testosterone production, which in turn can help you build muscle.

Supersets

Combining two exercises for the same muscle will do tremendous things for growth. Not only will it help you achieve a mind-blowing pump fast, spurring capillary generation, but new research suggests that it can also lower the pH of the blood and stimulate growth-hormone (GH) release. As European researcher Michael Gündill wrote in "The Science of Supersetting," in the August '97 *Ironman* (reprinted as Chapter 6 in this book), "Research shows that this type of training not only increases GH levels, but it also increases GH receptors located on the trained muscles." This is truly exciting research. Go for the burn and you'll definitely pack on mass faster.

CONNECTIVE TISSUE AND FIBER SPLITTING

What about items 4 and 5 on the list? How do you increase the amount of connective tissue and/or perhaps increase the number of muscle fibers?

Connective-tissue generation has to do with using heavy weights, so relying on the big compound movements—such as squats, dead-lifts, and rows—is key. Most hardgainers know that those exercises are best for mass stimulation, so they use them as the core of their workouts. In addition, stretch-position movements, such as sissy squats for quads and stiff-

bodybuilders know that this is the appropriate mass-building rep range and use it at every workout, so there's no real insight for the hardgainer there; however, item 3—increasing the number of blood capillaries—holds some real muscle-building possibilities.

Forcing blood into the muscle and inducing a pump causes new capillaries to form in the target muscle, which increases the muscle's size. How much bigger does the muscle get? It's hard to say because the percentage of increase may depend on genetics. Ah, but isn't this discussion about breaking through those barriers? Absolutely. So, here are a couple of things that facilitate the pump and force more capillarization no matter what your genetics.

Carbohydrates

While dietary carbs are getting a bad rap these days because of their association with insulin and fat deposition, you, as a hardgainer, shouldn't worry about that. Your blast-furnace metabolism won't allow for much fat storage, and any excess glycogen you can infuse into legged deadlifts for hamstrings, help increase connective tissue because they elongate the target muscle, creating more stress at the origin and insertion points.

As for increasing the number of muscle fibers, or hyperplasia, this is still a controversial topic. Some researchers believe it to be fantasy. Nevertheless, one animal study showed that muscle-fiber hyperplasia does occur as a result of—get ready—"stretch overload" (J. Antonio and W. J. Gonyea, "Skeletal Muscle Fiber Hyperplasia," *Medicine and Science in Sports and Exercise* 25: 1333–45 [1993]). The possibility of even small increases in the number of fast-twitch fibers is reason enough to use stretch-position movements. Another reason is fascial stretching.

LESS CONSTRICTION, MORE GROWTH

Stretch-position movements stretch the fascia, or the membrane that encases the muscle fibers. A looser encasement can mean there's more freedom for a muscle to grow because there's less fiber constriction. A good example of this constriction/slow-growth connection is the former Chinese tradition of binding girls' feet. Because tiny feet were considered attractive in the Chinese culture, wealthy families had their daughters' feet tightly bound for years at a time so that growth would be stunted—and it worked, although it was extremely painful.

Fascia can act in the same constricting manner and restrict a muscle's growth, according to a number of trainers and researchers, one of whom is John Parrillo. Parrillo suggests performing separate fascial-stretching sessions to facilitate faster muscle growth, but when you incorporate stretch-position movements into your routine, you don't need special sessions. The stretch-position movements do a good job of elongating the target muscles to the maximum and thus produce a fairly severe fascial stretch with each rep. To enhance the effect, you can hold the stretch-position of your last rep on these exercises for 5 to 10 seconds, but don't do this on every rep or you diffuse the myotatic reflex.

Ronnie Coleman.

UNLEASH NEW SIZE

One of the catch-22s of hardgainer training is that to build a muscle to extraordinary levels, you must train it from a number of angles, but when you do that, you can overstress your recovery ability and overtrain, which slows or halts growth. The bottom line is, if you want tremendous muscle growth in every bodypart, you have to figure out a way to use multiangular training without overtraining. Of course, many experts will tell you that all you need is one exercise per bodypart to get maximum development, but don't be fooled. It's just not that simple. If you follow that logic, you'll be using the hardgainer excuse for the rest of your days. The reality is that only certain fibers, those that have the best leverage during a particular exercise, will grow as a result of your doing that exercise, so you have to make sure the fibers contract in a variety of positions if you want to maximize the number of fibers that get total growth stimulation.

Here's a quote from Jaci VanHeest, renowned exercise physiologist at the United States Olympic Training Center in Colorado Springs, that will help you understand the need for more than one exercise per bodypart:

> Muscles contract when tiny levers on myosin, a muscle protein, fit into grooves on actin, another protein, and push it forward exactly like a ratchet wrench. But myosin can latch onto actin in any of several positions, not all of them ideal. Only when the myosin heads are in the right register can the muscle have the optimal tension. But optimizing every actin-myosin pairing is less an achievable goal than a Platonic ideal.

Essentially, that means almost every exercise optimizes a different configuration of actin-myosin pairings. While there's some overlap, you have to exercise a muscle in a number of positions to optimize as many of the actin-myosin pairings as possible.

After reading the foregoing, you may think that you, the hardgainer with limited recovery ability, are doomed. You can't possibly train every muscle from a variety of angles without smashing headfirst into the overtraining wall. Ah, but what if you were to use different exercises at different workouts to cover all the angles—say, in two workouts rather than trying to do all angles at one session? You would leap over your so-called genetic barriers and grow beyond your wildest imagination.

CONSTRUCTING THE ROUTINE

To construct the Ultimate Hardgainer Routine, we must first identify what "multiangular training" means. Each muscle essentially has three positions, or angles, that you should strive to train in order to optimize as many actin-myosin pairings as possible: midrange, stretch, and contracted. You may recognize this as Positions of Flexion, or POF. Here's a quick example using triceps:

> You train the midrange position with close-grip bench presses or lying extensions.
> You train the stretch position with overhead extensions—upper arms next to your head.
> You train the contracted position with kickbacks—upper arms behind the torso for a maximum contraction.

Note that you train three different points along the arc of flexion—from the overhead position to the hands-over-the-chest position to the behind-the-torso position.

This arc isn't as simple to define for some bodyparts, such as quads, but you can still put every exercise into one of those categories. Squats, leg presses, and hack squats are midrange movements because they do not completely stretch or fully contract the quads and they use synergy from other muscles to help the quads perform work. A sissy squat is a stretch-position movement for quads because the torso and thighs are on the same plane, and when the hamstrings and calves meet, the quads are completely stretched. Leg extensions are the contracted-position movement because the torso and thighs are at almost 90 degrees to each other and there is resistance in the contracted, or knees-locked, position.

On this mass-boosting program, you do the midrange and contracted exercises on Monday, and superset the stretch and midrange movements on Friday for an awesome pump and fiber hypercontraction. On Wednesday, you train arms, calves, and abs, hitting all three positions for most of these bodyparts.

One last point about triggering inordinate muscle growth. Researcher Michael Gündill explains how muscle soreness can enhance hypertrophy. His conclusion is that pure-negative sets can be very effective at inducing an anabolic environment but they should be used infrequently to avoid too much muscle damage. You may want to add a negative set here and there to this routine every so often. I highly recommend it. Changing the stress is one way to keep growth moving upward. Just don't get carried away with this technique or you'll undoubtedly overtrain.

Give the Ultimate Hardgainer Routine a fair trial, make adjustments where necessary, and you may be surprised at just how much easier it is to put on muscle. In fact, after you add slabs of new muscle to every bodypart, you may even be accused of being an easy gainer—by the other four finalists standing on stage with you waiting for the winner's name to be called.

Using stretch-position movements has a number of hypertrophic benefits, including the following:

Loosens fascial constriction to facilitate more fiber growth

Develops tendon and ligament size and strength

Increases neuromuscular efficiency for better fiber recruitment

May stimulate hyperplasia, or fiber splitting (this is still debatable from a scientific standpoint)

Here's a list of the best stretch-position exercises for each bodypart:

Quads: sissy squats
Hamstrings: stiff-legged deadlifts
Calves: donkey calf raises or leg-press calf raises
Chest: flyes
Delts: one-arm incline laterals
Lats: pull-overs
Midback: close-grip cable rows
Biceps: incline curls
Triceps: overhead extensions
Abdominals: full-range crunches

Incorporating these exercises into your routine—using correct form—at least once a week can significantly increase muscle growth.

WHAT, WHEN, AND HOW TO EAT FOR GROWTH

Eat-to-grow rule number one for the hardgainer is to feed yourself at least 20 grams of protein every three hours. Rule number two is to add some carbohydrates to your protein feeding—throw a banana into the blender with your protein powder, or eat some raisins.

Everyone knows that protein builds muscle tissue, but why eat carbs? Carbohydrates fill your muscles with glycogen so they'll pump to the maximum at every workout, and that facilitates capillary generation. Carbs also stimulate insulin, one of the most powerful anabolic hormones that the body produces, which may be the very reason teenagers crave junk food—it kicks insulin production into overdrive and teens grow. That's only the beginning, however.

A high-carbohydrate diet has also been shown to suppress cortisol. This is a stress hormone that can cause your body to eat its own muscle tissue. It's an emergency reaction from your body, a holdover from primitive times when the fight-or-flight mechanism was a must for survival.

For example, let's say you're living a few million years B.C. and you're in your cave, eating barbecued mammoth. A 500-pound saber-toothed tiger happens to catch a whiff of your meal and enters your cave for a bite. Of course, you've just polished off the last mouthful, and all that's left for him to fill his stomach with is you. Once you realize this, your adrenaline level skyrockets, giving you the ability to jump about 20 feet over the saber-toothed tiger, fly out the door of your cave, and then run like hell—right past a gazelle sprinting at full speed. This episode causes your body to pump immense amounts of cortisol into your bloodstream, which helps your system break down tissue, including loads of muscle, for immediate energy.

As a bodybuilder today, you want to minimize cortisol surges so that you avoid the catabolism they can cause. You say you don't confront saber-toothed tigers too often? Well, it's not just life-and-death situations that stimulate cortisol production, especially in high-strung hardgainers. Any stress can cause it, from high-intensity workouts to not eating to relationship problems to deadlines at work to final exams.

Hardgainers are especially susceptible to such cortisol surges, so in addition to a high-carb diet, a phosphatidylserine—or P.S.—supplement may help facilitate the muscle-building process. P.S. was shown in two Italian studies to suppress cortisol by up to 33 percent—which can create a muscle-building bonanza for ectomorphs. Champion Nutrition makes a P.S. supplement called Cortistat, and Muscle-Linc has its bestselling Cort-Bloc. Either of these is a great addition to the high-carb, medium-protein, medium-fat hardgainer diet that follows.

Other supplements worth a try include a whey protein powder, to make those three-hour feedings more convenient, and creatine monohydrate.

Creatine affects the anaerobic energy mechanisms in the muscle, which means it can help you train harder. It also helps increase muscle volume, possibly through water retention in the muscle cells. Reports of 10-pound muscle gains after just a few weeks of creatine supplementation are not uncommon, especially in athletes who don't eat a lot of red meat, a high-creatine food. There are a number of good powdered creatine products out there, including Twinlab's Creatine Fuel and EAS's Phosphagen HP.

Hardgainers should also take a good multivitamin/mineral supplement as well as the antioxidants—vitamins C (500 milligrams) and E (500 international units) and beta-carotene (20,000 international units). These compounds will help the body optimize its recovery ability and prime the system for spectacular hypertrophy.

Here's a good eating schedule, adapted from the 10-Week Size Surge Diet, that gives you about 3,000 calories, with 25 percent protein, 25 percent fat, and 50 percent carbs, along with a basic supplement program.

Meal 1
Milk (2% butterfat), 8 oz.
Oatmeal, 8 oz.
Egg whites, 2 (stirred into oatmeal)
Dates, 1/4 cup (about 5 whole dates)
Supplements: vitamin and mineral tablet

Meal 2
Whey protein powder in milk with
    banana

Meal 3
Roasted chicken, 6 oz.
Lima beans, 6 oz.
Rice, 1 cup
Sherbet, 3 scoops

Meal 4
Cottage cheese, 6 oz.
Pears (canned in own juice), 4 halves

Meal 5
Peanut butter and jelly sandwich
    on whole-wheat bread
Milk (2% butterfat), 8 oz.

Meal 6 (right after training)
Whey protein powder in milk with
  banana
Supplements: creatine, P.S. (cortisol
  blocker)

Meal 7
Tuna sandwich on whole-wheat bread
  (tuna packed in water)
Apple
Peanuts (handful)

Before bed
Supplements: P.S. (cortisol blocker),
  antioxidants (C, E, and beta-
  carotene), amino acid capsules

C. S. SLOAN'S GET-BIG RULES YOU SHOULD NEVER BREAK

1. Allow your system to recover. *Power Factor Training* author Pete Sisco has been saying for years that "Every workout is a kidney workout," and Mike Mentzer has said practically the same thing. The statement refers to the fact that your whole body must recover from a workout, not just the muscle group you trained. In other words, it makes no difference to your nervous system that yesterday was leg day and today is back day.

   That's the first thing people need to understand when they begin training or when they're not making gains. Overtraining is the number one culprit. If you're not making progress, make sure you're not working out more than three days a week—Monday, Wednesday, and Friday, for example. Also, you don't have to train your whole body on each day. Split it up, but don't train two days in a row.

2. Use the best exercises. There are good exercises, and then there are the best exercises. You should always pick the "best" exercises over the "good" ones. For example, pulldowns are good for lat width, but wide-grip pull-ups are

best. The bottom line is neuromuscular adaptation, or NMA.

   Muscles ultimately grow from stimulation to the nervous system—or perhaps don't grow because of too much stimulation (see item 1). The more neural activation you get from an exercise, the better the results. Generally, the harder the exercise, the more neuromuscular activation. That's why free weights are better than machines, and compound free-weight movements are better than isolation exercises with free weights. The best exercises are ones in which your body moves through space—squats, dips, chins, and deadlifts. Harder usually means best.

3. Change routines often. Your body is amazingly adaptive. The more advanced you are, the better your body is at adapting to workouts. Once your body adapts to the routine you're doing, growth stops cold in its tracks.

   Great bodybuilders have an innate ability to determine when they need to change things. Arnold Schwarzenegger was a master at this. He changed his routine almost every time he went to the gym—and his muscle growth was almost continuous.

   How often should you change your routine, and what type of changes should you make? After three to four weeks of the same training regimen, your body has adapted and you're ready for change. The reason your body adapts to your workouts is due to your nervous system, which learns to do an exercise more efficiently at each workout. Let's say you attempt a new chest workout this week. During the first week, since the stimulus is new, you might recruit 75 to 80 percent of your pec muscle fibers. At the next workout, you recruit a little less, and by about the fourth week, you may be recruiting only 40 to 50 percent of your pec muscle fibers. Now it's time for a new stimulus.

Research suggests that your body adapts to your choice of exercises the slowest. In other words, changing exercises is not as good as changing the manner in which you perform your workout. For maximum results, try a new workout style every three to four weeks. For example, do high-intensity, short-duration Heavy Duty workouts for four weeks, then switch to 10 sets of 10, then move to a Positions of Flexion program, and so on.

4. Pick your protein, and eat regularly. You can choose the best exercises, train correctly, and get enough rest between workouts, but if you don't consume sufficient calories and protein, then it's all for nothing.

The most important aspect of nutritional muscle building is consuming enough calories to facilitate the growth of muscle. Many bodybuilders fail to gain because they don't eat enough. Studies have shown that when people overeat, they not only gain fat, but they gain muscle as well. It's a big myth—albeit a widely accepted one—that when you eat too much, you only store excess calories as fat. You also gain a lot of muscle, so if you're a hardgainer, you need to eat the world.

Next to not eating enough, it's inadequate protein intake that prevents people from gaining muscle. Be sure to consume at least one gram of protein per pound of body weight, and $1^1/2$ to 2 grams is probably better.

THE ULTIMATE HARDGAINER ROUTINE

1. Each workout takes about one hour—with fewer than 20 work sets—which is perfect for the hardgainer's limited recovery ability. You can keep your intensity high without burning out.
2. There's a day of rest between workouts and then two days' rest at the end of the cycle, which facilitates systemic recovery.

3. The big compound movements are at the core of each workout—the first exercise for each bodypart on Monday and Wednesday, and the second exercise in the supersets on Friday. They train the mass of the target muscle and also help develop tendon and ligament size and strength.
4. The use of supersets and drop sets helps develop more capillaries in the target muscle and also can increase growth-hormone release. Plus, by using stretch-position movements as the first exercise in a superset, you kick the muscles into hypercontraction, which activates extreme fiber recruitment during the second exercise in the superset.
5. The use of stretch-position movements on Wednesday and Friday helps stretch the fascia to allow for more muscle growth, develops tendon and ligament size and strength, and produces more fiber recruitment through neurological stimulation and by placing the muscle in an emergency-response mode. Stretch overload may also cause hyperplasia, or fiber splitting, which can increase the growth potential of a muscle.
6. The rep ranges listed are ideal for activating type-2 muscle fibers, which are the fibers with the most growth potential.
7. By training each muscle from three distinct angles, or positions—midrange, stretch, and contracted—you optimize as many actin-myosin pairings as possible and therefore stimulate complete development in every target muscle.
8. Arms get only one direct hit a week, which prevents overtraining them. Remember, you get indirect arm work from all the pressing, rowing, and pulling at your other two workouts.

Monday
Quads and hamstrings

Squats or leg presses*	2 × 7–10
Leg extensions	1 × 7–10

Hamstrings

Leg curls*	2 × 7–10

Chest

Bench presses*	2 × 7–10
Crossovers	1 × 7–10

Delts

Dumbbell presses*	2 × 7–10
Lateral raises	1 × 7–10

Lats

Front pulldowns*	2 × 7–10
Stiff-arm pulldowns	1 × 7–10

Midback

Behind-the-neck pulldowns*	2 × 7–10
Forward-lean shrugs	1 × 7–10

*Do one or two light warm-up sets with 50 to 70 percent of your work-set weight prior to your work sets.

Bench presses.

Wednesday

Triceps

Lying extensions*	2 × 7–10

Superset

Overhead extensions	2 × 5–8
Kickbacks	2 × 5–8

Biceps

Barbell curls*	2 × 7–10

Superset

Incline curls	2 × 5–8
Spider curls	2 × 5–8

Deadlifts.

Leg extensions.

Overhead extensions.   Steve Cuevas.

Squats.   Ron Harris.

Calves superset

Donkey calf raises or leg-press calf raises*	2 × 10–15
Standing calf raises	2 × 10–15
Seated calf raises	2 × 12–20

Abdominals

| Incline knee-ups | 2 × 7–10 |
| Full-range crunches or Ab Bench crunch pulls | 2 × 7–10 |

*Do one or two light warm-up sets with 50 to 70 percent of your work-set weight prior to your work sets.

Friday
Quads superset

| Sissy squats | 2 × 5–8 |
| Squats or leg presses | 2 × 5–8 |

Hamstrings drop set*

| Stiff-legged deadlifts | 2 × 5–8 |

Chest superset

| Flat-bench flyes | 2 × 5–8 |
| Bench presses | 2 × 5–8 |

Delts superset

| One-arm incline laterals | 2 × 5–8 |
| One-arm dumbbell presses | 2 × 5–8 |

Cable crossovers.

Lats superset
Dumbbell pull-overs   2 × 5–8
Front pulldowns   2 × 5–8

Midback drop set*
Forward-lean shrugs   2 × 5–8

Note: Do one light warm-up set of each exercise before doing your superset. Also, stop your stretch-exercise work set a few reps short of failure, but push the second exercise till you can't get another rep in perfect form.

*To perform a drop set, do one set to failure, then quickly reduce the weight and perform another set to failure.

Incline curls.

Flavio Baccianini.

Chapter 5

COMPOUND AFTERSHOCK
SCIENCE-BASED TRAINING FOR ARMS

BY STEVE HOLMAN

Are you looking for a training routine that will inflate your arms to eye-popping proportions in record time—a program based on scientific principles and exercise analysis, so it absolutely, positively can't fail? Then, you've come to the right chapter. After only three workouts with the following Compound Aftershock Routine, your arms will feel fuller than ever before, and with some diligent effort, you'll eventually look as if you have 20-pound hams stuffed in your shirtsleeves—or perhaps 15-pounders, depending on your genetics.

How much discomfort must you endure for this transformation to occur? Well, the routines do require a high pain threshold, but the entire program takes less than 15 minutes.

We all need a little convincing before we start a new program, so here are five reasons this science-based arm program produces such spectacular results.

1. **It uses the most effective exercises.** According to the book *Muscle Meets Magnet* by Per A. Tesch, Ph.D., which takes an MRI look at which parts of leg and arm muscles are hit hardest by certain exercises, the movements in the Compound Aftershock superset hit the target muscle structures completely, rather than focusing on certain heads. Specifically:

Decline extensions—put maximum stress on the lateral, long, and medial heads of the triceps. You get total target-muscle stimulation with one efficient exercise. According to *Muscle Meets Magnet*, lying extensions on a flat bench, the most common version of this exercise, somewhat neglect the lateral and medial heads and focus on the long head. If you want to totally torch your tri's, do your extensions on a decline.

Overhead dumbbell extensions—also put maximum heat on all three triceps heads when you use two dumbbells. What's interesting is that the same movement done with a bar instead of dumbbells ignites only the lateral and medial heads, leaving the long head lagging behind. The reason the dumbbell version may be more effective is the fact that your palms are facing each other. The MRI analysis proves that varying your grip can have a substantial effect on target-muscle stimulation, as you'll see with the biceps exercises as well.

Close-grip barbell curls—put a total hit on the medial and lateral heads of the biceps. The brachialis muscles even get complete stimulation. If you do the exercise with a wide grip, however, MRI analysis says the medial head, the one closest to your torso, takes the brunt of the stress, and the lateral head and brachialis lag behind. Keep your grip close on curls, about 10 inches between your hands, and you'll get a more complete overall biceps hit.

E-Z bar curls.

Incline curls—sledgehammer the medial and lateral biceps heads once again. The unusual stretch you get on this exercise may be the reason. Keep your feet firmly planted on the ground, curl the dumbbells simultaneously, and don't pause at the bottom— change the dumbbells' direction immediately once you reach the complete stretch position to activate the myotatic reflex.

2. **The myotatic reflex, or prestretch, helps max out fiber recruitment.** This is especially true when you place the stretch exercise before a big midrange movement in a superset. For example, you can superset incline curls with close-grip barbell curls. Let's go through the entire Compound Aftershock biceps routine so you can see exactly how and why it's so effective:

- After a couple warm-up sets, you train the mass of the muscle with a heavy set of close-grip curls to failure; muscle synergy from your front delts makes this heavy overload possible.
- After a brief rest, you move to the Aftershock superset. First, you use incline dumbbell curls to trigger the myotatic reflex for some extraordinary fiber recruitment—a call to arms for the reserve fibers. With a preponderance of fibers in a heightened state, you immediately follow up with a lighter set of close-grip curls—about 20 percent lighter than your first set—so that synergy once again forces maximum fiber recruitment.
- After a two-minute rest and some massaging of your incredibly pumped biceps, you finish them off with concentration curls, one or two

Incline curls, start.

Incline curls, finish.

sets, squeezing hard for a count at the top of each rep for a peak-contraction effect.

Your biceps can't help but grow after this on-target attack.

Triceps get the same treatment:

- Do one set of decline extensions. It's OK if your upper arms move so that you get some synergy from your lats and teres muscles; just don't overdo it.

- Rest for a minute as you decrease the weight on the bar, then do one set of overhead dumbbell extensions supersetted with a second set of decline triceps extensions with the reduced poundage. Your triceps fibers will be screaming for mercy and pumped to the bursting point.

- Rest for about two minutes, and notice how your tri's are so full that they feel as if they're a couple of inflated tire tubes hanging from your rear delts. Now finish them off with dumbbell kickbacks, making an

effort to get your upper arms back past your torso on every rep as you contract your triceps hard. One set of this peak-contraction pain is all you have to endure—two if you're a real masochist.

3. **Better pump and burn.** New research suggests that supersetting helps lower the blood pH, which can force more growth-hormone release. These findings may verify why bodybuilders have been instinctively chasing the pump for years: it may be a growth stimulus, after all.

4. **Brachialis work for higher peaks.** The brachialis runs under the biceps, and when you develop this muscle, it can give your bi's more height, much as a developed soleus gives the lower legs more fullness. While close-grip barbell curls put a lot of stress on the brachialis, you may want to do one direct finishing set to give it that extra

jolt. *Muscle Meets Magnet* says incline hammer curls, with your thumbs up and palms facing each other, provide a focused hit on the brachialis.

5. **More recovery for accelerated growth.** You stimulate each target muscle to the maximum with only four or five sets, which means you have more recovery ability left for hypertrophy. Remember that the more sets you do, the more you deplete your system's ability to recover from intense exercise, so efficiency is key. Obviously, this is one heck of an efficient arm-building program, as you fatigue as many fibers as possible with as few sets as possible.

How should you use the Compound Aftershock arm routine for best results? An every-other-day split is the program that will help most intermediate bodybuilders make the best gains. Here's a sample:

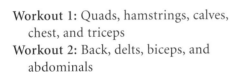
Concentration curls, start.

Concentration curls, finish.

Workout 1: Quads, hamstrings, calves, chest, and triceps

Workout 2: Back, delts, biceps, and abdominals

Always take a day of rest between workouts, and you have a recovery-oriented split that will produce impressive size increases.

If you prefer full-body workouts, a different approach is necessary, as follows:

Monday

Squats	2 × 8–10
Leg extensions	1 × 8–10
Leg curls	2 × 8–10
Standing calf raises	2 × 12–20
Seated calf raises	2 × 12–20
Bench presses	2 × 8–10
Pulldowns	2 × 8–10
Bent-over rows	2 × 8–10
Dumbbell upright rows	2 × 8–10
Full-range crunches	2 × 8–10

Wednesday

Compound Aftershock arm routine—you may want to do two supersets instead of only one, since you have more time to recover—or any arm-specialization program.

Friday

Same as Monday.

With this program, you train arms only once a week, on Wednesday, with the full Compound Aftershock Routine. Consequently, you may be able to get away with a few more sets, such as doing two supersets instead of one, but keep in mind that biceps and triceps get indirect stimulation on Monday and Friday from the pressing, rowing, and pulldown movements. This indirect work will pump blood into your arms for heightened recovery, but you want to make sure you don't overtrain. You'll see impressive results

from this type of program in a matter of weeks, guaranteed.

If buggy-whip arms is the disease, Compound Aftershock is the cure. Give this routine a try, and watch as your bi's and tri's swell to hamlike proportions in record time.

SEVEN TIPS FOR MASSIVE ARMS

1. When you train triceps and biceps on the same day, always do triceps before biceps. Pumped bi's can reduce the triceps' ability to reach a full stretch on certain exercises. For example, with pumped biceps, you tend to stop short on overhead extensions, which can diffuse the stretch reflex.
2. If you work arms along with other bodyparts, train them at the end of your routine. The indirect work from presses, pulldowns, and rows will help warm up your arms and prime them for the direct work to come.

Jean-Pierre Fux.

synergy, such as decline extensions and close-grip barbell curls. Those movements should be done with slightly looser form to bring muscle teamwork into play so that more target-muscle fibers will be stimulated.

7. Don't overtrain. Remember that your biceps and triceps get hit hard during presses, rows, pulldowns, and chins. Keep that in mind when constructing your arm routine. Doing fewer sets for arms is usually the best strategy when you're not specializing on arms.

3. Always work your brachialis—either with a specific exercise, such as incline hammer curls, or with a direct biceps exercise that also focuses on this muscle, such as close-grip barbell curls.

4. Use supersets periodically. You can achieve more growth-hormone release, a more extensive capillary network, and more muscle-fiber stimulation with this stress technique.

5. Eat some protein and carbohydrates every three hours. This keeps the muscle-repair process in motion, stuffs the bi's and tri's with glycogen for more volume, and prevents catabolism. If you don't eat every few hours, your body can cannibalize hard-earned muscle tissue.

6. Keep your form ultrastrict on all exercises except those on which you want

Weighted dips.

Frank Sepe.

Chapter 6

THE SCIENCE OF SUPERSETTING

BY MICHAEL GÜNDILL

Muscular training is by far the most powerful stimulator of growth-hormone (GH) secretion, and we know that a specific factor is responsible for all—or almost all—of the GH increase that occurs: the lowering of the pH of the blood.[1] In practice, that means the burning you feel during an exercise. Although we don't yet know all the reasons that a rise or fall in pH affects GH secretion, we do know one basic fact: the lower the blood pH, the greater the growth-hormone secretion. In other words, the more the muscle burns, the more the GH concentration in the blood increases.

Now, some people may suggest that in order to get a burning sensation in the muscle, you have to train it hard, so eventually your muscular gains will be due to more-intensive training and not to the rise in GH levels. That's true to some degree; however, it's important to understand that all intense effort doesn't produce a burn. For example, training very heavy—doing, say, eight reps on the bench press and giving 100 percent—won't make your pecs burn strongly. Often, you'll run out of strength before you feel a real burn. That

doesn't mean you didn't work your pecs and they won't grow.

On the other hand, doing a long set of light cable crossovers is likely to produce the most dreadful burn and, therefore, raise your GH level. Nevertheless, that type of exercise is not the most effective for making the pecs grow for bodybuilders who are not chemically assisted.

That may seem like a paradox, but let's examine the two examples in more detail. In the first case, hormones other than GH will induce muscular growth. Short, heavy, and intense exercise produces an increase in testosterone level.

In the second example, the muscular stimulation induced is weak despite an increase in GH. In other words, the muscle doesn't have a reason to grow, as it hasn't been sufficiently called upon or damaged enough (muscular microtrauma stimulates growth). The anabolic signal of the GH passes unperceived.

The point here is that in the first case, muscular growth would be greater if, in addition to the heavy set, you do a complementary

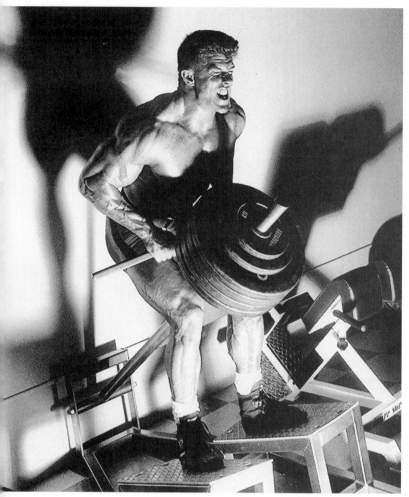

If you want optimal muscle growth from training, it's necessary to combine the two types of exercise.

in terms of anabolism. It's been established that GH is much more effective when cortisol levels are low. That means it's more effective to administer GH at night than in the morning. The phenomenon is reversed if cortisol secretion is blocked in the morning and if cortisol is then administered at night at the same time as the GH.

People who train at night generally have cycles of cortisol and GH secretion that are reversed, meaning that cortisol rises early in the evening and is lowered later by negative feedback, while GH levels are raised when the level of cortisol starts to decline, later in the night.

Cortisol is, therefore, a hormone that prevents GH from acting anabolically, so it's said to be catabolic. That brings us back to the question: Is it necessary to add exercises? The answer is no.

In fact, the harder you train, the greater the cortisol increase, both after training and overnight. Certainly, your GH level will be higher if you perform more exercises, but the GH will be negated by the cortisol.

exercise to make the muscle burn. If you want optimal muscle growth from training, it's necessary to combine the two types of exercise.

The question is, Does that mean you should do more exercises and more sets?

TAKE SOME LESSONS FROM THE EXPERIENCE OF GH USERS

Growth hormone is an expensive drug, so, to lower the cost to patients, for example, children who are abnormally small and people who don't secrete enough GH naturally, scientists have been searching to determine the moment the injections are the most effective

You can stimulate as much GH as you want—for free—but it requires an effort.

Postfatigue supersets

The second technique is based on the fact that it's easier to get a burn with the so-called isolation exercises than with the basic compound movements. For the uninitiated, a compound exercise is a movement that employs at least two different limbs—for example, the squat. All exercises in which only one limb moves are called isolation movements—for example, the biceps curl.

A postfatigue superset involves performing a compound exercise with heavy weights, then, without taking a rest, going to an isolation exercise that works the same target muscle—for example, bench presses followed immediately by cable crossovers. Of course, this postfatigue technique is even more effective when you use a drop set on the isolation movement.

Whatever technique you use, don't forget that the goal is to stimulate more growth hormone. You can stimulate as much GH as you want but it requires an effort.

The key is to find a way to combine the two types of stimulation—high intensity for more testosterone, lower intensity for more GH secretion—without increasing the duration of training. One solution is to reduce rest time. Following are two approaches that, while not the only appropriate techniques, are both excellent for accomplishing the objective.

Drop sets

It's difficult to make a muscle burn with a heavy load, but if you exercise to failure, then decrease the weight and continue, you'll quickly feel a burn. Dropping the poundage again and continuing will again increase the burn so that you can profit to the maximum. While you're enduring this process, don't think, "Burning equals pain"; think, "Burning equals growth hormone." Research shows that this type of training not only increases GH levels but also increases GH receptors located on the trained muscles. In other words, training increases the trained muscles' sensitivity to growth hormone.

Joe DeAngelis.

CONVERSION TO IGF

All of the foregoing information comes with an important caveat: If you want to gain muscle, raising the level of GH is only half the battle. Simply stated, it's not the GH that causes growth, but rather the transformation of GH to insulinlike growth factor, more popularly known as IGF. Therefore, the GH produced by training must be transformed into IGF in order to produce its miraculous effects.

Miraculous really is the word. IGF is currently very much in fashion—as a remedy for all the ills of people with diabetes, HIV patients, athletes, and people of advanced age. There's even a theory that IGF is 1,000 times more anabolic than steroids. In the bodybuilding world, many people believe that this substance will make its users explode with growth.

Is IGF more anabolic than steroids? In a test tube, the answer is yes. If that were really true, however, bodybuilders who don't use steroids could get as big as those who do,

since, unlike the situation with testosterone, it's relatively easy to make IGF levels go up. In practice, unfortunately, the answer is no. That doesn't mean you won't gain muscle by following the advice presented here, but you won't build as much muscle as a person who takes anabolic steroids. Anabolic steroids have very broad effects on several other key hormones in addition to interacting with the androgen receptors. Here are some examples:

Testosterone raises the level of IGF in the blood and also in the muscle (autocrine/panacrine action).

Nandrolone, contrary to what many believe, raises the level of free IGF by increasing its production and reducing the level of binding proteins that inhibit the action of IGF.

Trenbolone increases the sensitivity of the muscle fibers to IGF.[2] That means the minimal dose of IGF required to initiate anabolism is lowered.

NUTRITION IS THE KEY

The subject of IGF increase following a body-builder's training has been thoroughly studied in sports medicine.[3] In general, the results have been either deceptive or unproductive.

To begin with, it's easier to talk about converting GH into IGF than it is to accomplish it. The bodybuilders in the studies were either eating a diet more suitable for marathoners, or eating like so-called normal people. The fact is, it takes a combination of many elements to stimulate IGF production, including the following:

1. The total number of calories ingested should be increased so that there are no deficiencies either during the day or overnight.[4]
2. The level of proteins in the blood should be raised, especially the branched-chain amino acids (BCAAS).
3. The level of thyroid hormone, or T3, should be raised.

In effect, steroid-taking bodybuilders were already using IGF without knowing it. Thus, IGF will enhance muscle growth, but it's not so powerful that it will turn an average pro into the Incredible Hulk. Indeed, a simple injection of testosterone rapidly lowers the number of IGF receptors in the muscle. The addition of IGF, therefore, is superfluous, except for its effect in enabling a user to lose fat without losing muscle.

4. The level of GH should be raised.

5. The secretion of insulin should be optimal. This is crucial. A little insulin all day is essential, especially during training. That means taking in carbs during training—not too much to create hypoaminoacidemia, which is a lack of amino acids in the blood that's caused by too much insulin, and not too little, which will produce nothing. The solution is to stick with weight-gain products that are high in protein with only a moderate amount of carb to avoid hypoglycemia, or low blood sugar.[5]

Note that the increase of insulin during training won't prevent the rise of GH due to burning. In this case, GH increases because of a lack of oxygen in the blood and not because of low blood sugar.

While the preceding discussion doesn't represent everything there is to know about growth hormone and insulinlike growth fac-

tor, it should give you an understanding of their roles in training. Now you know why a burning sensation in the muscle is beneficial and why you should seek it out, along with a diet rich in BCAAS and a dynamic management of insulin levels.

References

1. W. Schmidt, "Effect of Exercise During Normonia and Hypoxia on the GH-IFG1 Axis," *European Journal of Applied Physiology* 71: 424 (1995).

2. R. E. Allene, "Trenbolone Alters the Responsiveness of Skeletal Muscle Satellite Cells to Fibroblast Growth Factor and IGF," *Endocrinology* 124 (5): 2110 (1989).

3. M. Terada, "Responses of IGF to Endogenous Increases in GH After Heavy-Resistance Exercise," *Journal of Applied Physiology* 79 (4): 1310 (1995).

4. G. B. Forbes, "Hormonal Response to Overfeeding," *American Journal of Clinical Nutrition* 49: 608 (1989).

5. R. M. Chandler, "Dietary Supplements Affect the Anabolic Hormones After Weight Training Exercise," *Journal of Applied Physiology* 76 (2): 839 (1994).

Gregory Reid.

Chapter 7

HARDGAINER'S CALL TO ARMS

BY STUART MCROBERT

Most trainees spend great chunks of their lives thinking about what they should be doing to improve their training, their diets, their supplementation. A lot of them, however, never get around to actually doing the kind of training they need. As a result, they never do what will satisfy them most—develop the body and strength that they crave. Successful muscle building is all about progressively adding poundages to lifts performed consistently and with good form.

You must live to add weight to each exercise. How many people actually focus on that goal? How many people in the gym where you train are instead concerned with the latest designer supplement or the latest gossip? The result is that the only people who make decent gains are those with terrific genetics or those who are stupid enough to take drugs.

Most people who read about abbreviated and basics-first training make only minor changes in their programs. They tinker a bit here and there, but they never really take the bull by the horns and make radical changes. Unless your training is going really well, start the program described here. It's designed to make you bigger and stronger all over. It's not a program for fat loss or to bring up a lagging bodypart. Most trainees don't need to fine-tune their physiques or get ready for a contest. Most just need more muscles.

Don't read through the program and find fault with it, or try to improve it. Have faith, and just follow it. A training schedule doesn't have to be perfect to work. For at least 10 weeks, just follow the program exactly as described. Do it. Don't put it off until next month or next year.

Before you start, take seven days off from weight training to give yourself a chance to recover from any overtraining you may have been guilty of.

THE PROGRAM

Train only two days a week: Monday and Thursday, Tuesday and Friday, or Wednesday and Saturday. Choose the days when you're most likely to perform at your best. If, for

Ofer Samra.

Workout 1

Squats or leg presses	2 × 8
Bench presses or parallel bar dips	2 × 6
Pulldowns	2 × 6
Grip work (see text)	
Crunches	2 × 15

Workout 2

Trap bar or stiff-legged deadlifts	2 × 6
Seated dumbbell presses	2 × 8
Barbell curls	2 × 8
Standing calf raises	2 × 15
Side bends	2 × 12
Grip work of your choice	

These routines are only the work sets. Warm up before each exercise. For the biggest exercises, do two or three progressive warm-ups, but for the smallest, a single warm-up set will suffice. For example, your warm-up

Roland Kickinger.

example, Mondays are your toughest days at work, don't train on Mondays. You need to be able to go to bed an hour earlier on your workout days to get in extra muscle-building sleep.

Perform two different routines, alternating them. You train twice a week but do each routine only once a week. As with all good routines, these are short.

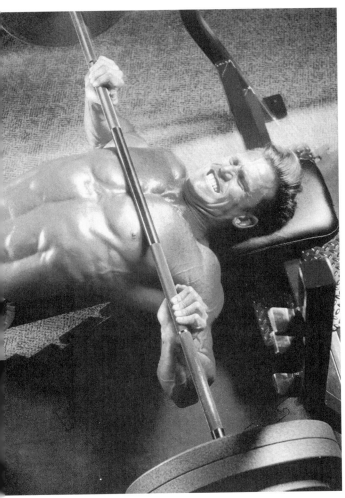

Lee Apperson.

sets for the bench press could be 135 × 10, 185 × 6, and 220 × 6 to precede two work sets of 245 × 6. For the barbell curls, though, a single warm-up set of 60 × 8 is adequate to precede work sets of 90 × 8. Begin each workout with five minutes of low-intensity stationary cycling, skiing, climbing, or skipping—until you break into a sweat.

For the grip work in the first workout, do holds, preferably with a thick bar. Take the loaded bar off the power rack pins as if you were doing the top part of a deadlift. Find a weight that you can hold for exactly 60 seconds. Rest for one minute, and then hold the same weight again. Your target is to hold the bar for 30 seconds on your second hold. Hold is actually the wrong word—try to crush it. Add a little weight each week, but make sure you hold for the full 60 seconds.

Take it relatively easy for the first two weeks to familiarize yourself with the exercises and practice good form. Push quite hard in the third week, and then start pulling out all the stops in the fourth. Thereafter you must push very hard at each session. Try your utmost to add a pound or more to each exercise each week.

Because you do the same reps for each set, the first set isn't as intense as the second. Rest for a few minutes between sets, long enough

Jonathan Lawson.

Ron Harris.

for you to do justice to the next set. When you can't make all of the reps on the second set of a given exercise, don't increase the weight until you can. If you add weight too quickly or too often, it will be your downfall.

Here's a sample progressive deadlift scheme, including the heaviest warm-up set:

> **Week 1:** 225 × 6, 250 × 6, 250 × 6
> **Week 2:** 225 × 6, 260 × 6, 260 × 6
> **Week 3:** 225 × 6, 270 × 6, 270 × 6
> **Week 4:** 240 × 6, 275 × 6, 275 × 6
> **Week 5:** 240 × 6, 280 × 6, 280 × 6
> **Week 6:** 240 × 6, 285 × 6, 285 × 6
> **Week 7:** 250 × 6, 290 × 6, 290 × 6
> **Week 8:** 250 × 6, 290 × 6, 290 × 6
> **Week 9:** 250 × 6, 292.5 × 6, 292.5 × 6
> **Week 10:** 250 × 6, 295 × 6, 295 × 6

POSSIBLE MODIFICATIONS

While some people respond well to different rep counts for a movement in the workouts, others don't. If, for example, you know that you don't respond well to sets of 8 but do respond to sets of 15 to 20, use the rep count that works best for you. "Best for you" is whatever lets you add weight regularly. If you don't know what's best, stick with the target reps suggested.

You may also need to adjust the exercises used in the workouts. Some people find it very productive to do squats and deadlifts on different days. They are overlapping exercises, meaning they work a lot of the same muscles. Others do better if they put both movements in one workout. That way, the glutes, lower

Roger Stewart.

Really push yourself in the gym. If you loaf, you'll make minimal or no progress.

back, and thighs get one hard session a week and have a full seven days to recover. So, if your deadlift or squat poundages grind to a halt, put the two exercises into one routine. (If you're doing leg presses and stiff-legged dead-lifts, though, you may find that it doesn't make much difference. There's nowhere near as much overlap in those two movements.)

The same approach applies to the bench presses or parallel bar dips in Workout 1 and the overhead dumbbell presses in Workout 2. If, when you are deep into the program, you find that your poundages aren't increasing, try putting the two exercises into the same work-out so that your shoulders get a full week's rest. When you rearrange your schedule, make sure you maintain the same number of exer-cises in each workout. If you move the dumb-bell presses to Workout 1, switch the pulldowns to Workout 2.

You may also need to use different exer-cises because you don't have the right equip-ment. If you don't have a pulldown unit available, substitute a prone row, chin, or one-arm dumbbell row.

TECHNIQUE

Good form is the bedrock of training success. Without it, your program is doomed to failure because sooner or later you'll injure yourself. What is good form? Well, it's not what you see in most gyms. Because I can't be with you to check your form or determine whether whoever advises you knows what he or she is talking about, I can only recommend that you get my book *Weight-Training Technique* and follow the advice in it so that you can look forward to years of injury-free, successful bodybuilding.

NUTRITION AND REST

Don't undermine the huge potential of this program by failing to give yourself adequate nutrition and rest. You must eat a high-quality diet packed with enough nutritious food to grow on.

Follow it up by getting to sleep early enough that you wake each morning of your own volition.

EFFORT

None of this will matter unless you really push yourself in the gym. If you loaf, you'll make minimal or no progress. To stimulate increases in strength, you must push yourself very hard on a consistent basis.

THE WRAP-UP

After you follow this program for 10 weeks, you may discover that you've made more progress than you did over the previous six months. When that happens, you'll know what productive muscle building is all about.

You'll get stronger, and your muscles will grow. You'll relish your training. You'll be fully rested between workouts. You'll pour maximum effort into each session. You'll see yourself progressing. This in turn will fire you up to train harder and better, and thus, you'll gain more. You'll be sore and a bit tired on your off days, but you won't be totally wiped out. Your appetite will increase because your body is growing and needs more sustenance. In short, you'll have found the Holy Grail of successful drug-free weight training.

You don't have to stop at 10 weeks. If the program is still working for you, keep doing it. You could get as much as six months of small but steady gains. That will add up to substantial improvement.

Now that you know how to train, put the knowledge to work. Deliver the unrelenting dedication, get growing, and become walking testimony to the enormous effectiveness of abbreviated, drug-free training.

Chapter 8

GIANT SPLITS
STRETCH YOUR ROUTINE FOR MAXIMUM RECOVERY AND GAINS

BY GREG SUSHINSKY

Bodybuilders want to get big. If you work out, that's what you want. You want muscle size—mass—but you don't always get it. Sometimes you follow the wrong routines or don't get proper nutrition, even when you know better. You may even look to things like steroids as your size-building solution.

You don't have to resort to steroids to get big—or make the mistake of following a champion's routine to the letter. That can be a highly unproductive route to the body of your dreams. There are better ways to go—and plenty of strategies for drug-free bodybuilders to put on muscle size. The giant, 10-day body-part split is one of them.

THE 10-DAY SPLIT

This routine takes the traditional concept of heavy training for muscle mass and improves upon it. It's for bodybuilders who have an adventurous spirit, who dare to try something a little different from what they're used to. It's for those who are less interested in the theo-

ries and the commonly used routines, those who desperately want to make gains, and even those who gain easily but want more. In short, it's for anyone who's interested in results. The bottom line of this routine is growth.

Here's the 10-day cycle. In effect, you use a five-way bodypart split, training on a one-day-on/one-off schedule:

Day 1 (Monday): Thighs and calves
Day 2 (Tuesday): Off
Day 3 (Wednesday): Back
Day 4 (Thursday): Off
Day 5 (Friday): Chest
Day 6 (Saturday): Off
Day 7 (Sunday): Shoulders
Day 8 (Monday): Off
Day 9 (Tuesday): Arms
Day 10 (Wednesday): Off

The cycle begins again on Thursday, when you repeat the program for Day 1.

The immediate reaction to this schedule is often a raised eyebrow. You don't train the muscle groups often enough, so how can the program work?

There are several reasons why this routine, which in theory and on paper doesn't appear to work, does work—and often works spectacularly. The key is the amount of rest and recovery time your bodyparts get.

HEAVY TRAINING AND RECOVERY

One of the requirements of gaining mass is heavy training. Many bodybuilders are successfully making gains these days by using heavy weights on basic exercises in fairly limited workouts. That's simple enough, and we all know it. Even so, most bodybuilders go through the process of starting out as beginners with the old standard three-times-a-week whole-body routines, then graduate to intermediate status, in which we begin to expand our workouts, adding exercises, sets, and repetitions, as well as weight. If we do this intelligently and carefully—and don't overdo it—many of us can continue to do well on it. Some gain better than others as we undertake this more extensive training. However, most of us eventually add too much and become overtrained.

The debates about training effectiveness often focus on the volume of training and, therefore, workout length versus the intensity, meaning whether you use heavy, medium, or light weights. Invariably, they overlook one significant factor: frequency of bodypart training. The fact is that when most bodybuilders move from a whole-body workout to a split routine, we go from working the muscle groups three times per week to twice. The switch from training three times a week to four, five, or even six times virtually guarantees it. So, we usually end up working out more often but pushing back the frequency with which we train each muscle group.

The drop in bodypart training frequency contributes a great deal more to sustaining gains than you may realize. No matter how much heavier or lighter you're training, no matter what additional intensity or lack of it you're using, this change in frequency is an extremely important, nearly hidden (in plain sight) principle for growth. The slightly longer rest between the times when you hit each muscle group adds to short-term recovery, and better recovery is a vital ingredient in the recipe for muscle growth. In addition, the fact that you continue working the other muscle groups provides an element of active rest and indirectly contributes to the recovery of worked areas because of the light pump—meaning increased circulation—that the resting areas are receiving.

FURTHER REFINEMENTS TO THE BASIC SPLIT

When gains stopped coming and/or chronic training fatigue set in on programs that work the muscle groups twice per week, some enterprising bodybuilders pioneered the every-other-day split, in which they work the muscle groups roughly twice every 8 to 10 days instead of twice every 7 days. Some power-lifters rediscovered the technique of working their lifts once a week, and some similarly enterprising bodybuilders have also tried working muscle groups once a week. That kind of workout has slowly grown in popularity over the past 10 or 20 years, as many who have used the approach feel they can make substantial gains and prolong a growth cycle. That's something for drug-free bodybuilders especially to keep in mind.

WHY LESS FREQUENCY WORKS

As noted, decreasing the frequency of body-part training dramatically improves the rela-tionship between the stress of training and recovery. In practical terms, if you train a bodypart hard every Monday instead of every Monday and Thursday, or instead of every Monday, Wednesday, and Friday, those days when you're not working the bodypart con-tribute additionally to the recovery process, which in turn boosts your actual muscle growth. What's more, the shift in frequency will automatically promote more intensity of stress in the workouts.

For example, if you do bench presses only once per week instead of twice, your pecs, tri-ceps, delts, and any smaller, auxiliary muscles affected, such as those in the upper back, get more rest than they would if you work them two or three times per week. Consequently, the next time you do benches, you'll automatically be more fully recovered than usual, and you'll probably be stronger and able to handle more weight than you would if you were benching twice per week. In addition, your energy will have increased from the extended rest, so you'll probably be able to do additional sets or reps—or, if you choose not to, you'll deplete less of your energy reserves for subsequent workouts. Because of the longer rest-and-recovery time between chest workouts, you'll gain more muscle mass than you would ordinarily, as you allow the body's process of overcompensation induced by exercise, which we call growth, to operate more completely—and even several days longer—than previously. As a result, you're more likely to gain more mass.

Continue to repeat this minicycle of better recovery leading to harder and more efficient workouts for a successful mass-gaining cycle. Bodybuilders who try training their muscles less often discover to their pleasant surprise how well the technique can work.

Note that what I'm talking about here is heavy training. If you keep the other stress factors—poundages, sets, and reps—light or moderate, a two- or three-times-a-week-per-bodypart training schedule is fine, but it's not the most effective for maximum recovery if you train very heavy. In that case, the best course is to drop the frequency and get maximum recovery for growth.

THE NEXT STEP

The giant split takes the previous concept even further. You can train muscle groups even less frequently than once per week and often get even better results. Try working the muscle groups every 10 days. You'll notice the difference in your workouts—particularly in the squats, benches, deadlifts, and other large-muscle exercises—in terms of how much harder you can train and how much more you can gain. You may wonder why you were squatting twice a week before.

EXERCISES, SETS, AND REPS

As you can see from the following routine, you work each bodypart separately, except for calves, which you work with thighs, and ab work, which you add to one or two of the workouts in the five-way split. Make sure you eat sufficient calories to gain mass, as this is a power bodybuilding routine and you may find yourself pushing and exceeding your old personal limits. Even so, the idea isn't just to get stronger, although your strength doubtless will improve. You simply want to build the maximum muscle you can for the work you're putting in. To that end, the exercises, sets, and reps have been carefully selected.

Calf raises.

Day 1: Thighs and calves

Squats	10 × 10, 8, 6, 4, 2, 2, 4, 6, 8, 10
Calf raises	10 × 20, 16, 12, 10, 8, 8, 10, 12, 16, 20

Squats.

Bent-over rows.

Seated behind-the-neck presses.

T-bar rows.

Day 3: Back

Deadlifts	5 × 10, 8, 6, 4, 2
Rows	5 × 10, 8, 6, 4, 2

Day 5: Chest

Bench presses	10 × 10, 8, 6, 4, 2, 2, 4, 6, 8, 10
Crunches	5 × 15–25

Day 7: Shoulders

Seated behind-the-neck presses	10 × 10, 8, 6, 4, 2, 2, 4, 6, 8, 10

Day 9: Arms

Curls	5 × 10, 8, 6, 5, 4
Lying triceps extensions	5 × 10, 8, 6, 5, 4
Crunches	5 × 15–25

Bench presses.

Curls.   Craig Titus.

WORKOUT TIPS

Use heavy weights. On most exercises, as indicated by the rep sequences in the routine, you work up in poundages and then back down, doing a full pyramid. It will be extremely challenging, but make sure you don't go to failure, instead coming within a rep or so of failure on your heavy sets. Because you expend so much energy on this workout, you have to make sure you leave yourself with a small energy reserve to get through the routine. Doing the heavy pyramids—including sets with as few as two reps—and going to failure would be too much for most bodybuilders' nervous systems.

Crunches.

Lying triceps extensions.

MODIFICATIONS

If you do the workout right, you won't have to do reps to failure or use any other intensity techniques. If you can't do the full 10 sets without exhausting yourself, or if you feel you aren't recovering, try a half pyramid instead of the full one, dropping the reps and increasing the poundage over five sets. Just don't add sets or reps. Ten sets per muscle group every 10 days doesn't look like much, but you'll proba-

bly be handling weights you never thought possible, and you'll be working extremely hard.

Hardgainers

The giant-split program can work wonders for hardgainers. Underweight, undersized trainees who desperately seek mass and strength will recover better and find this routine more productive than their typical two- or three-times-a-week-per-bodypart training. If you're a hardgainer, though, you'll almost certainly have to cut the sets back, and you probably can't handle the heavy weights on two- or four-rep sets as well as strong, easy-gaining bodybuilders can. That's no problem. Just cut the sets and poundages back to what you can do. If the two-rep sets are too difficult, try to keep the four-rep sets, or use three or five—whatever you can do that's in line with the principles of this routine. Necessary modifications that make a program work for you are always in order, but don't make changes without giving the program, as written, a fair try first—and don't cop out because you don't feel like working that hard.

Easy gainers

If you're extremely strong and energetic and you gain mass easily, you might want to try more sets. Easy gainers may feel as if they're not doing enough or not working their bodyparts often enough on this program. If you're one of those fortunate folks, try to resist the temptation to alter the workout too much. It might be better simply to add another exercise for each bodypart—say, one for shaping. Do it judiciously, then wait a few weeks until your body adjusts to the new workout, and see how you gain and recover. Some easy gainers find success by choosing workouts that are productive for trainees who have less potential and using them efficiently.

Ordinary bodybuilders

Most of us can be considered ordinary bodybuilders, if we're lucky enough that we're not outright hardgainers. Here's a recovery secret that can help you make maximum gains: Just because you feel that a muscle is recovered a few days after you worked it doesn't mean you have to work it again at that time. Recovery is often more subtle than you think, involving both short- and long-term processes, and if you wait slightly longer, sometimes you can work a muscle group even harder at the next session. The traditional concept that muscles recover in 48 to 96 hours has always been an oversimplification. (This hints at intriguing possibilities for pushing back the frequency even more, but for this discussion we'll stick with the 10-day program.)

Other modifications

If you feel you can't go very heavy at every session, use slightly lighter weights in some of the workouts, and your body will probably feel like going heavy again the next time. You won't have to force the intensity—or you shouldn't—as you'll most likely have the desire to train hard and heavy at every workout due to improved recovery and energy. What's more, knowing that you have to do squats, for example, only once in every 10 days will probably enable you to concentrate hard and give it your all.

There are also other rep, set, and exercise schemes you can use on the 10-day split, but, again, we're sticking with the main program here.

DIET

Don't bulk up, as so many bodybuilders still do, and call it mass. It's fat. Instead, if you try to gain only 5 to 10 pounds or keep your bodyweight close to what it was when you began the program—one of the most difficult things to do on a heavy mass-gaining regimen—you may find yourself acquiring lots of size without gaining a lot of bodyweight. It's not impossible—and what you get is very close to pure mass. In any event, try to make sure that any weight you gain is solid mass because the heavy training doubtless will have you wanting to eat much more.

WHAT YOU CAN EXPECT

You'll be sore from working hard and heavy, but you'll also stand a chance of breaking some of your personal records on exercises in the workout. You may also be surprised to find yourself experiencing fewer injuries, as working muscle groups too often is a subtle way of setting them up for damage.

There's so much more to say about the use of recovery for maximum growth and about the many ways you can adapt this type of program, but the foregoing giant-split routine should give you plenty to start with. It might alter your ideas about proper workouts—and the limits of your potential. You might find yourself growing as you never thought you could, putting on more mass than you ever thought possible.

Ronnie Coleman.

Chapter 9

SIZE MADE SIMPLE
BLAST YOUR BODYPARTS WITH ONE EXERCISE PER MUSCLE GROUP

BY C. S. SLOAN

Exercise programs come and go, and some even stay around for a while. Every now and then, an old lifting technique is revived because some researcher declares it's the ultimate way to put on muscle size—partial reps, for example. An old system may also get new life because a certain bodybuilding star uses it. That was the case when Dorian Yates revived Mike Mentzer's Heavy Duty training. Five years ago, no one trained that heavy. Things changed overnight when Dorian started talking about his training.

One training system that hardly anyone uses today is due for a revival: the one-exercise-per-muscle-group technique. No champs are touting its effectiveness in magazine articles. No one uses it in this modern age of multiple exercises. Even so, it's not likely you'll ever find a better way to train for size.

A principal benefit to using the one-exercise-per-muscle-group technique is that it works well with a number of bodybuilding programs. Probably the best feature is that you don't lose your pump. You know how that goes: You're training really hard on an exercise

and getting an excellent pump, when you decide to move on to another exercise; the next thing you know, the pump is gone and your workout goes downhill from there. Have you ever thought about just sticking with that exercise for 6, 8, or maybe 10 to 15 sets?

This training style is also excellent when the only thing you want is sheer muscle mass. Several champs have used it almost exclusively, and their progress was remarkable. The most prominent example is Sergio Oliva. The three-time Mr. Olympia's favorite way to train chest and back was to alternate sets, performing one for his chest and one for his back. The trick was that he stayed with only one exercise for each muscle group, primarily bench presses and chins.

Oliva would pyramid his weight on the two exercises. On bench presses, for example, he'd start off with a light weight and work up to a heavy triple, double, or single on about his 10th set. From that point on, he'd reverse-pyramid, dropping weight and adding reps.

Now, Sergio was no slouch in the genetics department. He'd probably have grown muscle

Tom Platz is also a proponent of one-exercise-per-bodypart training. He often performs up to 30 sets per exercise. On back, for example, he usually does T-bar rows for a full hour, using sets of 6 to 100 reps. The key to his success with this technique is that he allows at least seven days of rest before he blitzes the same bodypart again.

The point of these examples is that the one-exercise-per-bodypart routines are some of the most effective you'll ever find for working any of your muscle groups.

THE PYRAMID/REVERSE-PYRAMID SYSTEM

Pyramiding, then reversing, is the technique that Sergio Oliva used. When it comes to adding bulk and power, I don't believe it can be beat. You can either work one muscle group until you complete all the sets or alternate antagonistic muscle groups the way Sergio did, using what Platz calls jump sets. Either variation is great. Here is a sample routine for the bench press in which you work straight through before going on to the next bodypart. Note that the weights listed are only hypothetical, to give you an idea of the jumps.

Set 1: 135×12
Set 2: 185×10
Set 3: 205×8
Set 4: 225×6
Set 5: 245×4
Set 6: 265×2
Set 7: 275×1
Set 8: 225×6
Set 9: $205 \times 8\text{--}10$
Set 10: $185 \times 8\text{--}10$
Set 11: $135 \times 12\text{--}15$
Set 12: $135 \times 12\text{--}15$

no matter what routine he performed. However, he did prefer this style above all others.

Reg Park is another legend of bodybuilding who liked to train this way. He believed it to be the ultimate for building mass. He'd pick one exercise for whatever bodypart he was working and just hammer at it, using 6 to 10 reps until that bodypart was engorged with a monstrous pump.

If you feel that you grow better with fewer sets, then you don't need to perform so many. Just make sure you're warmed up well before you jump to an extremely heavy set. Also, don't try a heavy single or double every time you lift. You'll only burn yourself out. It's best to hold a little back most of the time. That

Hisashi Kamisawa.

keeps you from overtraining and also keeps you hungry for the iron at every workout.

Another variable that makes this particular routine effective is that you perform a wide range of reps, which ensures that you hit every muscle fiber. Every once in a while, you might try some really high reps on your final two to four sets. I'm talking the 20-to-50 range. That type of training helps build your blood vessels, capillaries, and neuromuscular pathways, which are needed for a huge pump.

HEAVY, MODERATE, LIGHT DROP SETS

You've no doubt heard of drop sets. They're also called strip sets, down-the-racks (when used with dumbbells), and descending sets.

Most of the time when people incorporate drop sets, they tend to let their reps drop with each drop in weight. The most effective way to perform these, however, is to maintain your reps or increase them as you decrease the weight. Popular International Federation of Bodybuilders (IFBB) pro Eddie Robinson trains that way almost exclusively. He claims it's the best method he knows for adding mass. Eddie picks one exercise and performs it for only four drop sets. Most of the time, he finishes each bodypart in about eight minutes.

If you think you can handle that, try Eddie's system. Pick a single exercise and do three or four heavy sets that drop from heavy to moderate to light, and see how tough you really are.

BURNOUTS

Perform one exercise for an all-out war with no mercy. That's the philosophy behind burnouts. Paul DeMayo regularly shocks his muscles with this single-exercise technique, and it's hell—so, consider yourself warned.

The best way to do burnouts is with a training partner. If you haven't got one, you'll need one. Pick one exercise, and challenge each other with what DeMayo calls "burn-downs." Take turns going back and forth until

Pulldowns, start.

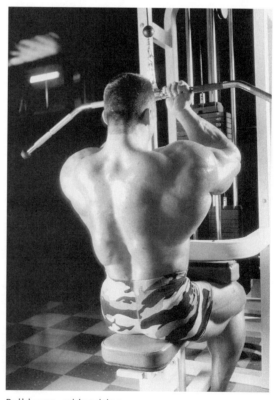

Pulldowns, midposition.

Pulldowns, finish.

Leg curls, start.

Leg curls, finish.

you can get only one or two reps. The trick is to keep the action moving. Your partner starts his or her set as soon as you finish yours, and vice versa.

If you decide to do this with either squats or—God forbid—deadlifts, be sure you have what Platz calls a "breathing bench" nearby. That's a bench for you to lie on between sets, gasping for breath.

10 SETS OF 10

The 10-sets-of-10 approach is probably the most common one-exercise-per-bodypart routine, and for good reason: it works. Vince Gironda has touted this training technique for years because, he says, it's probably the single best way to train, and it's really helpful in bringing up a lagging bodypart.

When using this approach on any bodypart, don't start out with your heaviest

poundage for 10 reps. Pick a weight that you can probably handle for a few more reps. The trick here is to hold your rest between sets to less than a minute, preferably 30 seconds. You're guaranteed a monstrous pump from this workout.

AND IF ALL OF THE ABOVE HASN'T CONVINCED YOU

Here's a little information about one-exercise-per-muscle-group training that you may not have known: The great Arnold Schwarzenegger, when he wanted to blast a particular muscle group into oblivion, would perform this kind of workout. Once a week, he and a training partner would drive into the country with some weights, limiting the workout to one exercise. As he described it in *Education of a Bodybuilder*:

> The first day we carried 250 pounds into the forest and did squats for three hours straight. I began by doing 20 repetitions with 250 pounds, then my partner did

whatever he could. Then it was my turn again. We ended up doing something like 55 sets of squats. The last hour was endless. Our thighs pumped up like balloons. That first day we gave our thigh muscles such a shock that we couldn't walk right for a week . . . and each of us put something like an eighth or a quarter of an inch on our thighs.

Now, Arnold took this to a maniac level. He and his partner always brought girls with them, and after they finished their shock training, they'd guzzle wine and beer, have a barbecue, and get drunk. As Arnold put it, "We carried on like the old-time weightlifters . . . sometimes it became pure insanity."

But it worked.

Bent-over rows, start.

Bent-over rows, finish.

Barbell curls, start.

Barbell curls, finish.

Dumbbell presses, start.   Bertil Fox.

ONE-EXERCISE-PER-BODYPART WORKOUT

It's winter and you're looking for a routine that will pack on some serious mass before T-shirt weather arrives in the spring. The one-exercise-per-bodypart routine will pack it on and pack it on fast—if you're consistent with it for the next two to three months. Are you ready? Here it is:

Monday and Thursday

Squats	5 × 10, 8, 6, 5, 4*
Leg curls	5 × 8–12
Standing calf raises	5 × 12–20
Seated calf raises	5 × 12–20
Full-range cable crunches or Ab Bench crunch pulls	5 × 8–12

Tuesday and Friday

Bench presses	5 × 10, 8, 6, 5, 4*
Incline bench presses	3 × 8–12
Under-grip pulldowns	5 × 10, 8, 6, 5, 4*
Bent-over rows or cable rows	5 × 10, 8, 6, 5, 4*
Dumbbell upright rows or dumbbell presses	5 × 10, 8, 6, 5, 4*
Barbell curls	3 × 8–12
Lying triceps extensions	3 × 8–12

*Your first 10-rep set should be light enough to count as a warm-up, then pile on the next poundage and go for broke on the four sets, adding weight after each set.

Dumbbell presses, finish.

Chapter 10

MASS VERSUS STRENGTH
TARGET-TRAINING YOUR MUSCLE FIBERS

BY BRENT ALLEN

The human body is a very complex machine, one that can specifically adapt to different types of training. For example, fast-twitch muscle fibers, those with which bodybuilders are most concerned, can be divided into two types with specific training protocols:

1. **FOG (fast, oxidative, glycolytic).** This type has the ability to utilize oxygen at a more efficient rate, thereby enabling it to contract quickly and be somewhat fatigue resistant. It also has the greatest capacity for size increases.
2. **FG (fast, glycolytic).** This type is better suited for pure power events such as the shot put and limit attempts in power lifting.

It has been conclusively demonstrated that fast-twitch muscle does have the ability to transform from FOG to FG with power training, and vice versa with bodybuilding training.

FAST-TWITCH COMPARISON

The training methods for strength and muscle mass are similar in that they must both include resistance work at an elevated intensity level; however, FG, or strength, fibers require a significantly higher intensity. You get the best twitch response from strength-oriented fibers when you emphasize acceleration in the concentric, or positive, portion of your repetitions. It also appears that you get a higher twitch response when you use compound movements, or exercises that involve two or more muscles in conjunction, such as squats. The repetition range for FG-fiber training is one to six, and the fewer the repetitions, the more FG isolation you get.

If you're a bodybuilder, you want to stress primarily the FOG fibers. To do this, you must also train hard, but it's more of a paced high intensity. The FOG fibers, due to their somewhat fatigue-resistant qualities, need more repetitions. Eight to 15 appears to be the optimal number for building muscle mass.

Even so, it's actually the time the muscle spends in maximal exercise that's the true determinant of the primary fiber type. For optimal strength development, it appears that the exercise should be around 90 percent anaerobic, or no more than a total of 15 seconds of actual performance time during any work set. For muscle mass, the optimal energy production is 66 to 85 percent, or between 25 and 75 seconds of performance time.

For example, if you perform a set of only six repetitions but include an isometric contraction at the top of each rep as well as emphasizing the negative, or eccentric, phases, that could triple the tension time on the muscle, thereby making it a FOG-dominant, or bodybuilding, exercise.

If, on the other hand, you perform those six repetitions with very short pauses between them to allow the muscle to recover somewhat, rather than keeping constant tension on it, and you focus on acceleration, you stress the FG fibers, making it more of a strength-building set.

If you're interested in muscle mass, your primary concern should be total tension time—at a maximal-paced intensity—rather than counting repetitions. Remember, each set should last 25 to 75 seconds.

Strength trainers should concentrate on quick, explosive sets with a short rest/pause between repetitions. It also appears that work sets performed for submaximum repetitions with short rest periods between sets—one of the basic concepts of the Bulgarian training style—specifically target the FG, or strength, fibers.

Bent-over lateral raises, start.

Bent-over lateral raises, finish.

Bent-over rows, start.

Bent-over rows, finish.

Seated cable flyes, start.

Seated cable flyes, finish.

Seated cable flyes, finish.

Upright cable rows, start.

Upright cable rows, finish.

Dumbbell flyes, start.

Dumbbell flyes, finish.

RECRUITMENT OVERLAP

In simplest terms, to target FG, or strength, fibers, you perform your repetitions in a certain way—focusing on acceleration, with the set lasting about 15 seconds. To target FOG, or muscle mass, fibers, you focus on keeping tension on the working muscles for 25 to 75 seconds and working till fatigue sets in.

Keep in mind that there's significant overlap between the two fiber types. For example, some FG-specific training will aid in mass development due to the increase in strength and increase in recruitment of muscle fibers. Also, some FOG-specific training will aid in strength development based on the increase in muscle size and endurance.

FIBER-TYPE COMPARISON

Train FG (Strength/Power) Versus FOG (Muscle Mass)	
FG (Strength/Power)	**FOG (Muscle Mass)**
Emphasize acceleration	Emphasize sets to failure
Perform each repetition like individual singles, with a rest/pause between repetitions	Use more continuous-tension time for each individual repetition and between repetitions
Train with maximum intensity	Train with paced intensity
Do 6 or fewer reps per set	Do 8 to 15 reps per set
Maintain a core time per set: 15 seconds (this is work time, not rest time)	Maintain a core time per set: 25 to 75 seconds (this is work time, not rest time)
Use a heavier average resistance	Use a lighter average resistance

Chapter 11

HIGH-INTENSITY TRAINING

BY ELIOT JORDAN

Regular readers of *Ironman* magazine are familiar with the philosophy of high-intensity training espoused and popularized by Nautilus inventor Arthur Jones and more recently by his disciple, former Mr. Universe Mike Mentzer. A variation of the system is also favored by former Mr. Olympia Dorian Yates. The concept of training each set to momentary muscular failure is a key aspect of this approach.

According to the tenets of high-intensity training, muscular gains don't come from sheer volume of training but instead from factors such as set-by-set intensity and the amount of weight used. This philosophy represents the classic overload concept in the purest sense: You must stress a muscle with heavy weights to induce hypertrophy, or growth, then allow sufficient time for full recovery. The result should be a body that compensates for the induced stress by gaining additional size and strength.

Jones and Mentzer frequently point out that sprinters show considerably greater muscular mass than long-distance runners, such as those competing in marathon events. The simple explanation for this morphological variation is that the sprinters train more intensely; that is, they do more work in a given period.

Many of the Jones-Mentzer principles are based on what Jones refers to as self-evident logic. If you've read his colorful articles in *Ironman* over the years, you know he's not impressed with most academic exercise researchers, who conduct their experiments in the form of double-blind studies. Jones maintains that it's not too difficult to rig such studies to obtain desired results.

One principal aspect of the high-intensity training that reflects self-evident logic is the idea of training to failure. Mentzer and Jones consider this essential in inducing muscular size and strength. They point out that the human body has a finite recovery ability, and the less you tap into this recovery ability, the greater the gains.

Recovery ability is just another way of explaining the stress and compensation theory originally stated by scientist Hans Selye.

Incline dumbbell presses, start.

Incline dumbbell presses, finish.

Seated dumbbell presses, start.

Seated dumbbell presses, finish.

In short, you impose stimulation sufficient to stress the body without exhausting its ability to recover. The body will then compensate for the imposed stress by changing something. In the case of exercise, this change involves additional protein synthesized in myofibrils or muscle fibers. As a result, the muscle grows.

The problem is finding the right level of stress; in other words, how do you impose enough exercise on the muscle without stepping over the line? According to Jones, if you overtrain, you'll exhaust recovery ability. That leads to either no gains or a catabolic state, in which you lose previous gains. Jones and Mentzer's solution is twofold: (1) Use heavy weights to stress the muscle fibers most prone to hypertrophy, the type-2B fibers; and (2) train to momentary muscular failure.

Training to failure, according to the high-intensity school of thought, makes sure you stimulate the type-2 muscle fibers while using up the smallest amount of your delicate recovery ability. Over the years, Jones has amended his ideas concerning the proper frequency and volume of training to promote maximum progress. When he first appeared on the scene in the early 1970s, he suggested training no more than three times a week, averaging two sets per exercise. More recently, he favors no more than one set per exercise.

Mentzer has refined the system to the point that some of his trainees hit a muscle only once every eight days (see his book *Heavy Duty II*). Again, the idea is to allow sufficient recuperation time while minimizing the expenditure of existing recovery ability.

Critics point out that the recovery-ability concept is nebulous. Scientists trained in subjects such as statistics have problems with something that can't be precisely quantified. Jones and his followers answer that training to failure ensures maximal muscle stimulation for everyone, regardless of individual differences, while preventing overtraining.

In a review of training to failure published in a 1996 issue of the journal *Strength and Conditioning*, the authors say that it's more important to use heavy weights than it is to train to failure. They cite past research indi-

cating that, according to the majority of studies, multiple sets are superior to single sets when it comes to inducing muscle size and strength gains.

Dumbbell lateral raises, start.

Dumbbell lateral raises, finish.

Weight lifters, the authors say, rarely train to failure, yet are undeniably strong. The review also states that consistently training to failure often results in overtraining in about three to four weeks. This is a curious outcome, considering that the whole idea behind one-set-to-failure training is to avoid overtraining. The scientists say that the cumulative muscle damage imposed by training to failure sets the stage for injuries because of the increased fatigue you experience when you train to failure regularly.

The review concludes by suggesting that if you want to try training to failure, you should do it as part of a periodic program for no more than three weeks at a time.

Arthur Jones would doubtless use one word to describe the authors of this study: idiots. If anything, the greater rest featured in current high-intensity-training programs would tend to increase recovery while minimizing injuries due to more complete muscle and connective tissue recovery. On the other hand, I've observed that high-intensity devotees like Dorian Yates appear to have frequent

injuries, such as Yates's elbow, biceps, and shoulder problems.

As anyone who's trained with heavy weights for years knows, however, injuries are an occupational hazard. In defense of Yates and other high-intensity-training proponents, there's no proof that he could have avoided his injuries if he'd trained in a more conventional style. In fact, I've heard Yates say that he's especially careful to warm up his muscles before tackling the heavy sets.

As I see it, the main problem with high-intensity training is not injuries. To get maximum benefit from one set, you really must train to failure. That's easier said than done. In my experience, few people have the mental intensity to train to utter and complete failure. They may think they're doing it, but the reality veers considerably from their fantasy. People who do only one set without reaching true failure will make gains only if they're rank beginners.

Another possible—and rarely discussed—drawback of high-intensity training is that you

Deadlifts, start.

Deadlifts, finish.

must cut your calories drastically to lose body-fat. Since the average high-intensity routine takes about 20 minutes, you probably burn only 100 to 200 calories at most. Both Jones and Mentzer aren't in favor of additional aerobics, noting that such exercise will adversely affect recovery ability and either limit or prevent progress.

Thus, if you're seeking to lose bodyfat on a high-intensity workout, you need to eat about as much as a 90-pound gymnast. I do recall, however, that Mike and his brother Ray, a former Mr. America, did plenty of aerobics in their bodybuilding heyday. I don't think either Mike or Jones has addressed the problem of calorie and fat loss in terms of the present incarnation of high-intensity training. That said, however—and as an anecdotal aside—I can report that I made the best gains of my more than 30 years of training while using a program similar to the one advocated by Mentzer and Jones. I used no drugs and trained only two or three times a week but gained tremendous strength. I was accused of being on the juice, yet I took nothing but natural food supplements. Contrary to what some experts would predict, I suffered no injuries and certainly increased my muscle size and strength.

I eventually stopped using the system—not for physical reasons but due to psychological factors: while my workouts were short,

after two straight years of high-intensity training, I eventually couldn't stand the thought of having to train to failure with ponderous poundages at every workout. In retrospect, I think the solution would have involved using the system during one phase of a longer program. In that respect, I agree with the conclusion offered by the training-to-failure review: True training to failure is most efficient as part of a year-round periodization system.

Cable curls, start.

Cable curls, finish.

Aaron Baker.

Chapter 12

MASS MANIA
RADICAL ROUTINES FOR SHOCKING SIZE

BY C. S. SLOAN

I've written quite a few articles in *Ironman* on the best techniques for making your physique huge, powerful, freaky, and superstrong. The bottom line is: mass is still king. You can talk all you want about proportion, symmetry, shape, and definition—they're all very nice—but size rules above everything.

Size is what keeps hard-core bodybuilders motivated. It's what drives them day in and day out to be the best they can be. If size isn't one of your goals, then you're not a hard-core bodybuilder.

Over the years, I've learned many things from all kinds of bodybuilders, from pros to up-and-coming amateurs to local gym rats who work nine-to-five jobs but crave more mass. The following routines are among the techniques I've picked up. You may have seen some of them before, or maybe you discovered one of them on your own (there's a tendency among great instinctive trainers to be able to do this). I guarantee, however, that they aren't the run-of-the-mill, high-volume—or even low-volume—workout you've been used to.

POWER-STYLE JUMP SETS

I've written about jump sets before, but you rarely, if ever, see anyone actually performing them at your local gym. It's a pity. Jump sets may be the best technique around for becoming large and in charge. They let you remain strong for your entire workout and take plenty of rest between sets while still giving you a pretty damn good pump.

I first read about jump sets in an article by Leo Costa, the creator of the Serious Growth training system, but I'd actually seen someone doing them years before. In a small gym where I trained in the 1980s, there were several big bodybuilders and powerlifters, but one guy towered above them when it came to immense size. I remember seeing him work chest and back one day and thinking that his training technique was rather odd. He'd do a set of bench presses, wait two to three minutes, do a set of wide-grip chins, wait another three minutes, and do another set of benches. He was always strong and never seemed to get weaker on any of his sets.

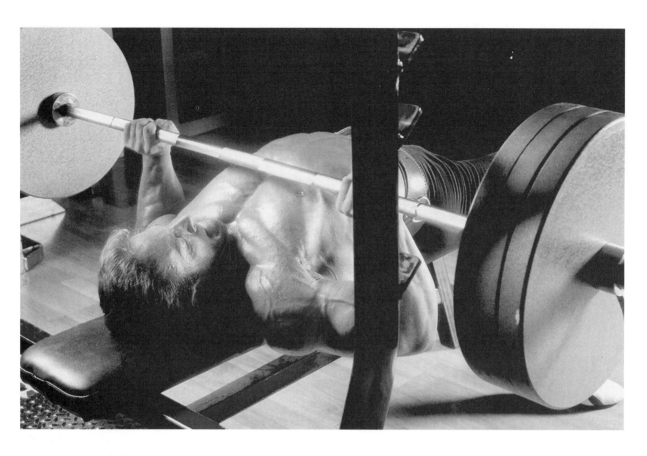

At my next workout, I decided to give this technique of what appeared to be a lazy form of supersets a try. After slowly alternating a few sets of bench presses and bent-over rows in that manner, I couldn't believe how strong I still was. My reps never dropped on my benches; in fact, they increased a little on my third and fourth sets. What a workout for mass and power! Since then, it's been one of my favorite forms of lifting.

Why is this technique so terrific? In the 1970s, Arthur Jones found it to be an effective way to train. The reason is simple: When you activate the agonist muscle groups during a set and then do a set using the antagonist muscle groups, the antagonists contract more strongly than they would if you hadn't done the agonist set first.

You can train all agonist-antagonist muscle groups in this manner. Chest and back, quads and hamstrings, front and rear delts, and bi's and tri's all work well with jump sets. Give them a try. You'll be glad you did.

BURNOUTS

If you train with a partner, burnouts will help you achieve some of the best workouts of your life. They give you an awesome pump, and if you try them with an exercise as difficult as squats, you'd better be prepared.

I started including burnouts in my program at the recommendation of my training partner. We'd decided to do barbell curls, and my partner tossed out the idea of doing a set and then, without setting down the bar, handed it to me. When I got through my set, I was to immediately hand the bar to him. We gave it a go. In this balls-to-the-wall manner, we did as many sets as we could, constantly tossing the barbell back and forth without stopping, until we could no longer curl it for a single rep. It was pure torture. My partner claimed that the workout put a quarter of an inch on his arms. I don't know if that's really true, but I do know that burnouts are an awesome way to get an out-of-this-world workout.

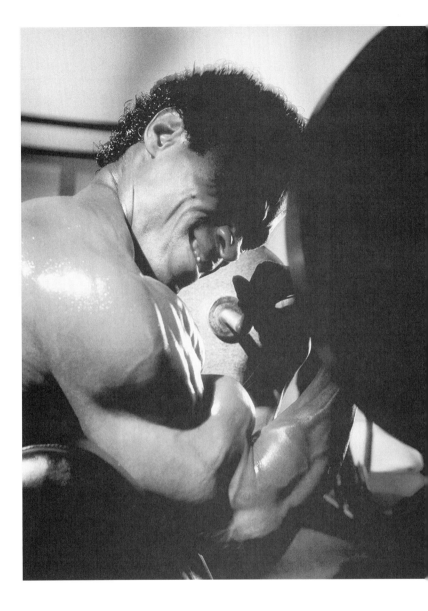

As Kevin Levrone likes to say, "Intensity builds immensity." That statement is definitely true with burnouts.

STAGGERED-VOLUME TRAINING

I stole this one from Douglas Christ, an exercise physiologist who believes that staggered-volume training—call it svt—is the ultimate technique for maximum growth-hormone release. I don't know if it's the best form of training you can do, but it might be a nice

exercise for at least 12 reps each, and do your sets in a semi-jump-set fashion. After you've done, say, four sets for your chest, do four for your back and then return to chest for another four sets, and so on. Alternate all opposing muscle groups in this manner.

Don't throw in any intensity techniques or take any sets to failure; instead, stop one or two reps short. The sheer volume of work will take care of making your muscles hypertrophy.

The SVT workouts aren't easy. They require a lot of dedication if you're going to make it through a complete whole-body routine; however, they're a nice break from ultra-heavy workouts because you use moderate weights, which don't tax your nervous system as much as heavy weights.

break for a few weeks if you've been performing the low-volume, heavy-duty style workouts that are in vogue today.

There are three key factors to this workout:

1. It's a whole-body routine, so you train only three days a week—or less—taking at least a day of rest after each training session.
2. You pick only one exercise for each bodypart. In other words, you do just squats for your quads, benches for your chest, wide-grip chins for your back, and so on. You want to pick the more difficult exercises over the easier ones, since you use just one per bodypart. So, stick with the basics; forget about leg extensions, flyes, lat pulldowns, concentration curls, and other isolation movements.
3. You do a high volume of work to stimulate more growth-hormone release. Perform at least eight sets per

STATIC CONTRACTION TRAINING

I think Mike Mentzer was the first to recommend this next type of lifting. If you've read any of his work or the work of John Little and Pete Sisco, then you've heard about it before.

Static contraction training is nothing new. In the 1970s, when Mentzer was a competitive bodybuilder, both he and his brother Ray used what they called isometric holds. Whether you call it an isometric contraction or a static contraction, it's all the same thing.

When performing a static contraction set, you don't move the weight through a range of motion. You simply hold a heavy weight without moving it. For example, for bench presses, you pick a weight that you can hold in the contracted position for, say, 15 seconds before it starts to drop on its own accord. The next time you work out, either you increase the amount of weight and try to hold that for 15 seconds, or you hold the same weight for 20 seconds.

Mentzer recommends performing one static hold followed by a slow negative in the same set. He claims that this type of workout really helped a lot of his clients start to grow

again at the rate they'd been experiencing before they hit a plateau.

Mentzer recommends doing only one exercise for one set—or at the most, two sets—per bodypart. I think you'll get even better results in terms of muscle shape and size if you use three or four different exercises for only one set apiece.

You may have noticed that most pro bodybuilders who claim to follow Mentzer's principles—like Dorian Yates, Phil Hernon, and Jean-Pierre Fux—don't use the Heavy Duty system exactly as Mentzer prescribes. They all do anywhere from three to six exercises per bodypart, performing only one set to total failure, plus warm-ups. That's anywhere from three to five more sets than Mentzer would recommend.

Here's an example of a static-contraction chest workout:

Flat-bench flyes (warm-up) 2 × 15
Bench presses
1 15-second static contraction hold followed by an eccentric contraction
Incline presses

1 static hold in the power rack with no
  negative
Pec deck flyes or cable crossovers
1 static hold in the contracted position
  followed by two eccentric contractions

There you have it: one hell of a static contraction workout. At every other session, you might want to add a set or two of an exercise done in a traditional manner followed by a forced rep or two.

ONE EXERCISE, PURE INTENSITY

I stole this idea from Tom Platz, the king of quads. Platz brought a whole new level of intensity to training. The man still regularly cranks out one-exercise-per-bodypart workouts, in which he performs up to 30 sets on each movement. As if the sheer volume isn't enough, he also takes each set to a psycho level of intensity. Platz wouldn't think of stopping a set when he reaches momentary muscular failure. He wholly believes in doing forced reps, negatives, or static holds at the end of a set. Platz says his muscles will either grow or fall off the bone.

Recuperation is the key here. Platz waits two weeks before he trains the same bodypart with such an intense workout.

There are benefits to working out in this manner, even if you do it only occasionally. Here are a few examples of situations in which you'd want to use what Platz calls total-exhaustion workouts:

1. To bring up a lagging bodypart
2. To shock a muscle into new growth
3. For variety and a total change of pace—some people don't change their workouts around enough

If you do decide to try Platz-style training, make sure that you do it only occasionally. You can get too much of a good thing. Also, be sure to include at least two days of rest after such a workout. Your body will need the time to rest and recover so that it can grow.

OTHER FACTORS

Aside from good training, there are a few things you should do to make your workouts more effective. The most important factor in

Double-biceps cable curls, start.

getting good results from your workouts is recuperation. The following is a pretty good bodypart split for maximum recovery:

Day 1: Legs
Day 2: Biceps and triceps
Day 3: Off
Day 4: Chest and shoulders
Day 5: Off
Day 6: Back
Day 7: Off
Day 8: Cycle begins again

Don't worry that you're taking a week before you train a bodypart again. You won't shrink. If you do the kind of high-intensity workouts described here, you'll need the rest.

Double-biceps cable curls, finish.

Start.

Finish.

Of course, if you use the SVT workout, you won't use the split because you'll be performing a whole-body routine three times a week. Variety is the key. You may want to switch to the SVT program after several weeks of high-intensity training. For example, you might perform static contraction workouts for four weeks, followed by power-style jump sets for another four weeks, and then, to give your body the rest it needs, switch to the lighter, high-rep SVT program for two to three weeks.

That's very similar to what gargantuan Jean-Pierre Fux does. After six to eight weeks of high-intensity training, he does a high-rep total-body workout three times a week for three weeks. He says that it really helps his recovery system and he always comes back stronger after the whole-body cycle.

The other extremely important factor is diet. If you don't get enough calories and protein, you're not going to build muscle—period. All of the great bodybuilders past and present understood the importance of nutri-

tion. Larry Scott says that nutrition is 80 percent of your physique. I couldn't agree more.

If you're really an ectomorph—that is, a hardgainer—then be sure to eat plenty of calories. Don't believe that crap about needing only 2,500 calories a day to grow muscle. That's just for endomorphs. You'll be better off consuming 25 to 30 times your body-weight in calories every day. So, if you weigh 180 pounds, you need anywhere from 4,500 to 5,400 calories to grow muscle. Eat big to get big. Also, try to take in at least one gram of protein per pound of bodyweight; two to three grams is an even better plan. That means lots of chicken, steak, milk, eggs, and tuna.

If you're interested in piling on some mass, make use of these innovative workout techniques. Remember that your training doesn't have to be boring, and, besides, the longer you've been working out, the more variety your body needs. So, hit the gym, get wild, and fuel the machine.

Chapter 13

HOW TO TURN 10 GOOD EXERCISES INTO EXPLOSIVE MEGA-MASS BOOSTERS

BY STEVE HOLMAN

Some exercises pack mass on just about anyone. Take the squat, for example. You have to be pretty handicapped in the leverage department to squat for any length of time without gaining some appreciable muscle. It trains your entire body, not just your legs, to grow bigger and stronger. The same goes for the deadlift.

Other exercises, however, take some tweaking if you're going to get the most stimulation from them—triceps pushdowns, for instance. Some bodybuilders can slam out set after set with a straight bar and not feel a damn thing happening. When they switch from a straight bar to a rope, including a twist of the wrist at the bottom of each rep, it's as if somebody stuck white-hot horseshoes under the skin on top of their triceps.

How do you know if an exercise is a waste of your time? The answer is pump and sensation. If you get a pump in the target bodypart and you have the sensation that the muscle is going to explode after a few sets, the exercise is stimulating growth. On the other hand, if you have a hard time determining which

bodypart you're training with an exercise, it's time to either look for a new movement or try a variation.

One little technique tweak can make an exercise 20 times more effective. Here are 10 basic movements that you can turn into mega-mass boosters with simple variations or substitutions. If you decide to try them, make sure your partner is standing by with a fire extinguisher to douse the incredible burn.

1. LEG EXTENSIONS

Finishing off the quads with leg extensions is a common practice, and for good reason: you get resistance in the contracted position, which makes the muscle fibers almost burst through the skin. Most bodybuilders know that to get the most out of leg extensions, they should flex their quads hard at the top for a count. If you want an even better contraction—and to make those quad fibers really scream—try to raise your thighs off the seat during that part of the rep. You probably

2. BENT-OVER ROWS

Many bodybuilders turn bent-over barbell rows into a completely new exercise, the half-assed deadlift thrust clean. They bring their upper body to an almost upright position as they heave the bar into their waist—or worse, their upper thighs. That doesn't work the back—at least not the midback, which is the primary target. If you really want to attack your midback, grab a pair of dumbbells and lean forward, resting your chest on an incline bench or other support. Now do strict rows, squeezing your scapulae together at the top of each rep. Be sure to keep your arms angled away from your torso so that you don't hit too much lat. This exercise will thicken your back and etch in detail that you didn't think you could ever achieve there.

Leg extensions.

won't succeed, but that's not the point. It's the attempt that makes the difference. One or two sets of leg extensions in this style, and you may need a walker to get to your next exercise.

Bent-over rows.

Low cable rows.

Supported dumbbell rows.   Mike O'Hearn.

3. CROSSOVERS

When you do standing cable crossovers, you have a cable handle in each hand, and the cables are attached to heavy weight stacks that pull your arms up. It's almost impossible to keep your torso still when you pull the handles down in front of your waist. That's the problem with cable crossovers: you get a whole lot of swaying going on, which tends to bring the front delts into play, and that minimizes chest involvement. Try dragging a flat or decline bench over to the crossover apparatus and attaching the handles to the low hooks. Now recline on the bench with a handle in each hand and, with a slight bend in each arm, pull until your hands touch above your sternum at the upper end of your rib cage. That will give you much better pec isolation because your torso can't move. Remember to keep your chest high and squeeze those pecs hard on every rep. And don't let the weight stacks drop. Perform the reps slowly, and try to keep tension on your pecs throughout the range of motion.

Cable crossovers.   Robby Robinson.

Decline cable crossovers.

4. BARBELL SHRUGS

Ask a bodybuilder what the problem is with barbell shrugs, and the answer will be, "The damn bar drags against my thighs." That's only part of the problem, however. When you use a bar, your hands can't move freely, which limits your range of motion and your muscle gains. A better way to zap your traps is to shrug with dumbbells and shoot for an enhanced range of motion. Start with a forward lean and the dumbbells touching in front of your thighs, with your shoulders down and stretching your traps. As you shrug, allow the dumbbells to move out to your sides. When your traps are fully contracted, the dumbbells will be at the sides of your thighs, parallel to each other. This gives you more scapulae rotation and thus more trap stimulation.

Dumbbell shrugs, start.   Chris Faildo.

Barbell shrugs.

Dumbbell shrugs, finish.

5. STANDING CALF RAISES

One of the big reasons bodybuilders have trouble building calves is that they don't pay attention to the negative, or eccentric, phase of each rep. Because of the skill you develop in walking and running, your calves are very efficient when it comes to performing work. That means you have to force them to do something to which they're not accustomed—like controlled negatives. On each rep of your standing calf raises, keep your knees locked, drive up into the contracted position, then count to three as you lower the weight. Do this on every rep. Yes, you'll probably have to decrease your poundage somewhat, but your calf growth won't suffer in the least; it will kick into high gear.

Speaking of suffering, be prepared for some ungodly soreness for the next few days after you perform these sets with negative emphasis. You may want to try them one leg at a time for even better results. According to the book *Muscle Meets Magnet*, which uses magnetic resonance imaging to explain how exercises affect leg and arm muscles, the one-leg calf raise hits more of the overall calf than the two-leg variety.

Calf raises.

6. UNDER-GRIP PULLDOWNS

Most bodybuilders keep their bodies perpendicular to the floor when they do under-grip pulldowns. That style, however, tends to put too much stress on the biceps at the expense of lat contraction. To remedy this, you can either try to lean back so that your torso is close to a 45-degree angle to the floor when you pull the bar to your chest, or try rope pulls. Hook a double-rope attachment to a low pulley, grab the rope with both hands, bend over until your torso is about 45 degrees to the floor, and pull the rope to your waist. Be sure to keep your arms close to your sides and squeeze the heck out of your lats at the top. Go for a scapular squeeze, and try to keep your torso as still as possible.

Under-grip pulldowns.

Concentration curls.

Double-biceps cable curls.

7. CONCENTRATION CURLS

Concentration curls are a great biceps movement. You can really focus on the peak contraction. Even so, you can get an even better contraction with another exercise.

First, you must realize that the contracted position for the biceps occurs when your upper arm is next to your head and your forearm is pointing downward, flexing your biceps. When you're in this position, you look as if you're doing a one-arm triceps extension, except your palm is down, twisting outward. You can see how the concentration curl doesn't quite get you there.

A better exercise is the double-biceps curl performed in the cable crossover apparatus. If you do these on your knees, you'll get even closer to the biceps' fully contracted position because you'll be pulling from more of an overhead position. This is one of the best exercises for finishing off your biceps training.

8. CRUNCHES

If you read *Ironman* on a regular basis, you know that the crunch is a good exercise for contracting the rectus abdominis, the rippled muscle on the front of your abdomen, but for best results, you should begin the exercise with your lower back arched. This prestretches the rectus abdominis and also brings into play the surrounding ab muscles such as the obliques and the transverse abdominis. The total impact of full-range exercise on abdominal development is tremendous, and the Ab Bench is the best way to get prestretch and total contraction for that chiseled-granite look from sternum to pelvis. Arch back, don't pause, then pull forward to a full contraction. You'll work your rectus abdominis from top to bottom and through a full range of motion, which means faster gains than you could achieve with inefficient half-range on-the-floor crunches.

Crunches.

Full-range crunches.

Ab Bench crunches.

If your gym doesn't have an Ab Bench, you can always use a high pulley and a preacher bench to simulate the full-range movement, but be sure not to overstretch. The Ab Bench prevents overstretch and spine compression, but with a cable setup, it's entirely possible to injure yourself if you're not careful. Remember, the key is the prestretch with an arched back, which standard crunches lack. [The Ab Bench is available from the Home Gym Warehouse, (800) 447-0008, ext. 1.]

9. STANDING LATERAL RAISES

Almost everyone who does lateral raises does them incorrectly. A strong statement? You bet, but it's the absolute truth. Here's how the faulty form goes: Stand, keep your arms bent, and heave the dumbbells up, with your torso taking on a pronounced backward lean as the dumbbells reach the muscles' contracted position. This is a great delt exercise—front delt, that is. To hit your lateral, or side, heads, you must lean forward and keep your delts rolled forward as well. This activates the important lateral head that's so necessary if you want to build that wide-as-a-barge look.

Most bodybuilders have trouble sticking with this form, however. For that reason, the best way to target your lateral heads for some radical new stimulation is to perform the movement while sitting backward on a high-incline bench. Try holding the dumbbells at the top for a count, for even better hypertrophy. If you can't stand reducing your poundage for this stricter version, do two sets of your regular "front-delt" laterals to satisfy your ego, and end with one set of these strict side-head burners.

Standing lateral raises.   Joe DeAngelis.

Lunges.

10. LUNGES

To perform standard lunges, you step forward with a weight across your shoulders, plant your foot, and bend your knee. Then you push off, step back, and step forward with your other leg. This can be somewhat dangerous if you lose your balance or you land too hard. A better way to lunge is to step back with the nonworking leg, instead of forward with the working leg. This allows you to focus on each slow negative as you lower into a lunge and turns the exercise into more of a one-leg squat than a knee-torquing balancing act. Plus, if you have a Smith machine, you can perform the exercise even more safely.

Smith machine lunges.

Chapter 14

POWER BODYBUILDING FOR SERIOUS SIZE AND STRENGTH

BY BRYAN E. DENHAM

In the past 20 years, weight-lifting equipment has undergone major cosmetic surgery. Expensive commercial machines have sent rusty iron plates and beat-up dumbbells to the corner antiques shop, while carpeted aerobics rooms and neon lights have turned the hardcore gyms of yesteryear into social clubs and fitness centers.

Many people enjoy this atmosphere—it's healthier than a smoke-filled bar, to be sure—but others want nothing more than to feel the gnarl of an Olympic bar and hear the rhythmic sounds of clanking iron. This advice is for them.

Sophisticated exercise machines do offer convenience and variety, but when it comes to building muscle density and hardness, they pale in comparison with the fundamental power movements. That's one reason that many bodybuilders today look ripped but not particularly dense. They rely on Smith machines and leg presses instead of barbells and dumbbells, and their physiques show it. Seldom do you see great spinal erectors and mature development in the major muscle groups, but you often see massive physiques that a safety pin could seemingly pop like a balloon.

Serious weight lifters—those who perform the core movements consistently over a period of years—simply have a different look from many of the folks whose pictures appear regularly in bodybuilding magazines. Our focus here is on the three movements performed at power-lifting meets—the squat, bench press, and deadlift—as well as certain productive auxiliary exercises, and the physique you can build by centering your training around them.

Cable crossover, start.

SQUATS

Barbell back squats are the ultimate leg exercise. Stepping out of the rack with hundreds of pounds on your shoulders, descending to the point at which your hamstrings begin to tighten, and exploding upward with unbridled force is weight lifting at its finest.

A problem that novice weight lifters sometimes experience when performing squats is the manner in which they begin the exercise. When you begin a squat, you can do one of two things: you can allow your knees to shift forward, thereby letting the bar move forward, or you can squat correctly by tilting your pelvis slightly up and back, keeping your knees directly over your feet to execute a safe repetition.

A lot of trainees are afraid that if they squat from their heels, as they should, they'll sit too far back and keep on going. While it's

Cable crossover, finish.

conceivable that a beginner might fall while performing a back squat, it's highly unlikely, especially if he or she has an experienced spotter nearby. If you haven't reached the point where you can perform every rep of a squat set with your knees staying directly above your feet, then you haven't learned proper form. Under no circumstances should you allow your knees to drift forward, as that will place undue strain on your joints. What's more, your poundages will never go up, for your exhausted joints will be able to handle only so much. If you struggle with squats, get yourself a good partner and practice sitting back on your heels with just a modest amount of weight on the bar. Don't allow the spotter to stand too close, as you want to feel comfortable in your space, but do ask him or her to pay special attention, because you'll be working on something new.

When you perform squats, concentrate on exploding upward, which engages the powerful gluteus muscles and enables you to keep your torso from slouching forward. Few bodybuilders ever perfect the barbell back squat. Typically, they convince themselves that squats are for powerlifters and skip the exercise

entirely, or they perform squats with technique that is simply pitiful.

Poor squatting technique comes from either using too much weight, limited hip and ankle flexibility, or refusal to accept constructive criticism. To maximize the effectiveness of a weight-lifting movement, you have to understand what's involved. For instance, when you descend to the point at which your thighs are parallel to the floor, you're doing something very natural. In contrast, when you load too much weight on the bar and stop halfway down, you're doing something very unnatural. At that point, you shift the emphasis from the major muscles of your legs and trunk to the joints, increasing the risk of injury. No one is impressed by lifters who load 600 pounds on the squat bar and move the weight two inches, as that basically amounts to a treacherous good morning. The thighs go nowhere near parallel, the torso slumps forward, and the weight is heaved back to the starting position.

Sweeps and muscularity are built by performing sets of full, flawless repetitions. That means controlling the weight throughout the set. Many lifters approach the squat as a one-dimensional exercise; that is, they descend to

Squats, start.   Justin Brooks.   Squats, finish.

parallel as quickly as possible and then drive the weight back up. While you don't want to do a negative here, you do want to feel your leg muscles at work. Dropping too quickly reduces the amount of work you must perform during the set, and it can also prove dangerous. If the weight is too heavy, you may find yourself dropping straight to the floor.

With respect to equipment, you should eliminate everything except a good power belt. Too many trainees use items such as knee wraps as a crutch to move weights that are too heavy to be handled properly. There's no need to alter the very natural movement by creating unnatural compression in your knee joints. While you may think you'll grow stronger if you wrap your knees, you'll actually become weaker. What can you lift without the bands?

Next, buy yourself a pair of good work boots with rubber soles and raised heels. Wear the boots when you do squats, and you'll be amazed at how strong you feel during the movement. The elevated heels keep your torso from slouching forward and also assist you in sitting back. Never perform squats in running shoes with cushioned soles; you'll lean forward to the point of tipping.

In addition, when you begin a set of squats, concentrate on locking the bar into your rear delts and stepping back with force. With squats, you really need to take charge of the bar and go to work. That doesn't mean yelling and making a fool of yourself in the gym, but it does mean concentrating and powering through your sets. Keep your back tight, and explode out of the hole with each repetition. Visualize yourself driving the weight instead of letting the weight drive you.

LUNGES

Barbell lunges are a great exercise for building mass in the glutes and quadriceps. Unfortunately, they're often performed improperly, and lifters seldom benefit from the exercise as much as they could with sound technique.

Unlike many trainees, I view the barbell lunge as a power movement; that is, I usually go very heavy and complete my work sets with

Lunges, start.

Lunges, finish.

Lunges, finish, alternate leg.

once you arrive. So, try not to make a habit of touring the gym when you do lunges. Instead, view them as an exercise that's similar to squats.

With respect to safety, don't try to impress your fellow trainees by showing them how far you can step out with the weight. That motion is very hard on the knees, and if you extend too far, you might end up on the floor. The body has natural ways of moving, and when you force it to do things that it isn't supposed to do, you increase your chances of injury. Try putting a broom handle on your shoulders and getting used to the feel of lowering yourself and coming back up. After a few minutes, you should notice a groove (i.e., a comfortable path of movement). Most exercises have such a path, and with the barbell lunge, you'll find it where the knee of the leg that's stepping forward stays directly above the foot. Don't allow that knee to extend across your foot, and don't keep it trailing behind by taking too large a step. Find your groove, and stay in it throughout the set.

DUMBBELL SQUATS

Here's another exercise for building explosiveness. Dumbbell squats are especially effective following squats, an exercise that sometimes leaves your lower back fatigued when your legs could stand additional work. I like to squat as heavy as possible, which means I place a great deal of strain on my back. Rather than injure myself by doing too many sets of barbell squats, I grab a couple of dumbbells and do four sets of eight reps. That takes my leg sessions to an entirely new level. So, instead of performing, say, 10 sets of barbell squats in your routine, try substituting a pair or dumbbells after you complete your seventh set.

Holding the bells at your sides with a hammer grip, descend as you would during a full squat, and drive back up from your heels. Keep the dumbbells at your sides throughout the set, and don't slam them off the ground at the bottom of your reps. To build explosiveness, you must avoid bouncing out of the hole and instead perform a series of fluid touch-and-go reps.

no more than eight repetitions—four on each leg. That means I don't step out as far as some people do, but my descent is full. I take the weight off the rack, get my feet set, tighten my torso, and step out with my left leg to the point where my knee remains directly over my foot during the repetition. When my left thigh is parallel to the floor, I power the weight back to the top. This movement requires strength, balance, and agility, which explains the reason barbell lunges are one of the best weightlifting exercises for competitive athletes. No matter what the sport—baseball, basketball, football, soccer—athletes in the elite ranks must have supreme body control, and lunges are an excellent means of developing it.

Walking lunges, which are commonly performed in glitzy health clubs, do little in the way of building and toning muscle. When you don't force yourself to drive the weight back to the starting position, you miss most of the benefit. It does take energy to control the weight as you descend forward, but it takes even more effort to explode out of the hole

Dumbbell squats, start.

Dumbbell squats, finish.

Bodybuilders should use wrist straps to allow their arms to hold the dumbbells as long as necessary. In contrast, football players and competitive deadlifters should not use straps, since there is much to be gained in grip strength as well as explosiveness from this exercise. For example, defensive backs in football must often lunge at a running back or wide receiver and throw the offensive player to the ground by his jersey. Too often, trainees consider only one facet of an exercise and disregard the other benefits it may offer. When you put together a training program, ask yourself what you hope to gain from each movement. With regard to dumbbell squats, use straps if you're trying to add detail to your upper-leg muscles by doing higher-rep work, but if you're trying to build a powerful grip for the jersey of an opponent or the handle of a 36-inch Louisville Slugger, skip the straps.

BENCH PRESSES

How much can you bench?

The answer to that frequently asked question depends not only on who the weight lifter is but also on what he or she considers a legitimate lift. Take a look around the gym and you'll notice that the bench press clearly means different things to different people. Which of the following matches your definition?

1. Lowering the bar as fast as possible, slamming it off the sternum, and heaving it back up.
2. Lowering the bar at a controlled pace, allowing it to touch your chest briefly, and then powering it back to the starting position.
3. Lowering the bar at a steady pace, resting it on your chest for a lengthy pause, and pressing it up.

For me, definition 2 applies. Of the many ways you can execute the bench press, the touch-and-go approach seems the most beneficial. By controlling the bar as it comes down, you build force in your upper torso and generate increases in muscularity. By allowing the bar to touch your chest briefly and then driving it back up, you develop power and explosion. In other words, you get the best of both worlds: strength and muscularity.

With regard to performance style 1 on the list, forget it altogether. That approach is for the uninitiated and the foolish. Number 3 should be reserved for people who train for power-lifting competitions, in which a lengthy pause is required.

Apart from the speed at which the bar should travel, there are some other points to bear in mind when you bench-press. First, make sure you understand how to position your body on the bench. Lie back on the bench, and position yourself so that your eyes are looking slightly to the front of the bar. Squeeze your shoulder blades together, and press them down toward your waist. That will elevate your chest and help isolate your pecs as much as possible. With a slight arch in your lower back and your butt on the bench,

Bench presses, start.

Bench presses, finish.

unrack the weight and begin the exercise, as just described.

When you bench, make sure to keep your hands just outside your shoulders. At no time should you place your hands completely outside the rings on either side of the Olympic bar. That concentrates most of the strain on a very small area of the outer pec—right where the muscle attachments are located. An ultra-wide grip doesn't do much in terms of development either, and it won't help you build strength. It might, however, help you suffer a torn pec. Remember to keep the movement contained and explosive.

DUMBBELL PRESSES

The dumbbell press performed on a flat bench is an excellent alternative to the traditional barbell press. It offers an excellent range of motion when done properly, and because you must control the 'bells throughout the set, the exercise helps you develop lifting coor-

dination. For beginners, coordination is paramount.

Perhaps the most common training mistake I see on dumbbell presses is the width at which trainees hold their arms. It's important to remember that dumbbell presses aren't the same as dumbbell flyes, so when you hear bodybuilders talk about "feeling the stretch," assume they're describing flyes performed with a modest amount of weight.

You should perform dumbbell presses with your elbows tucked in so that the 'bells rest on your pectoral muscles at the bottom of the movement. That helps engage the pecs and, more important, prevents the upper-arm bones from wandering into dangerous territory. When you do this exercise, concentrate on containing the dumbbells while keeping your torso locked on the bench.

As with barbell presses, squeeze your shoulder blades together when you lie back, then press them down toward your waist. Your chest will pop up, and you'll be in position to knock out some heavy reps.

Dumbbell bench presses, start.

Dumbbell bench presses, finish.

That brings me to my next point. For some reason, many lifters are under the impression that dumbbells are used only for shaping and toning—that they offer little benefit from the standpoint of power. I would argue the opposite: that sets of four to six reps performed with dumbbells will greatly enhance muscle density and help increase poundage on the barbell bench. If you want muscles that feel like stone, you have to lift weights that look like mountains.

INCLINE DUMBBELL PRESSES

Dumbbell presses performed on an incline bench are beneficial for the upper pectorals and front deltoids. They give you a greater range of motion than barbell presses, and they demand total control.

The most common mistakes that lifters make on this exercise include setting the bench at too high an angle, clanging the dumbbells together at the top of each repetition, and allowing the dumbbells to drift too far out, thus endangering the shoulder capsules.

The best angle for incline dumbbell presses is about 20 degrees. Raise the bench much higher, and you'll be doing the equivalent of shoulder presses. It's hard enough to isolate your pecs during chest training—the last thing you should do is decrease their role by increasing the workload on the front and side delts.

In addition, instead of clanging the dumbbells at the top of each rep, power them up with absolute control, and don't let them touch at any time. On the way up—and on the way down—maintain control and don't allow them to drift outside your shoulders. If you perform the exercise correctly, you'll notice that the dumbbells come straight down; they don't go astray. Push yourself, and don't ask for a spot on this one. Handle the dumbbells yourself, and learn to exercise perfect control.

Incline dumbbell presses, start.   Incline dumbbell presses, finish.

PARALLEL BAR DIPS

One of the best ways to develop strength and muscularity is to work with your own body-weight on exercises like this one. Not only will you work your pecs, delts, and triceps, but you'll also have to maintain body control and balance, which adds to the work being performed.

As with chins, the key to a good set of dips is to keep your body on the same vertical plane throughout the set. Also, you don't want to let yourself descend too far. The bottom part of a dip is very important in terms of safety; if you go too far down, you'll place a great deal of strain on your shoulders.

When you perform dips, lower yourself to the point at which you feel a slight stretch in your pectoral muscles. Lean very slightly into the stretch, and then push yourself up, remembering not to lock out at the top. Again, locking out is tough on the joints, and it also keeps you from working your muscles to the fullest. With each lockout, you throw the pressure onto your joints and off of your muscles. Keep your repetitions fluid, and maintain total control.

Weighted dips, start.

PUSH PRESSES

The development of Smith machines and other devices has helped to make push presses an exercise of the past. It's so easy to pull up a padded chair and glide through a set of overhead presses—why use your entire body to train the muscles of the upper torso?

By using your legs to help drive a barbell over your head, you can handle greater training poundages than you could with a machine press. That means you'll be able to build the kind of muscle density that machines can never produce—regardless of the company's advertising claims. Heavy free-weight exercises are on an entirely different level.

The key is to keep the barbell in front of your head instead of behind it. Behind-the-neck presses of any kind are dangerous, and with the added weight used on push presses, your shoulders are placed in a vulnerable posi-

Weighted dips, finish.

tion. When you keep the barbell in front, you reduce the amount of external rotation in your upper-arm bones, thus making the exercise safer and more productive.

As discussed for the bench press, never place your hands wider than shoulder width on the bar. The issue is not only safety but also the muscles being stressed. When you take an extremely wide grip on the bar, you can't involve your chest and shoulders as thoroughly as you can with a medium-width grip.

To perform push presses, drop into a half squat, with the bar resting on your upper pecs. Concentrate on keeping your spinal erectors flexed, and avoid hunching your back as you power the weight up. Don't lock your elbows at the top of the movement, as that can harm the shoulder sockets.

Push presses are a power-oriented exercise, and you should approach them as such. Even so, you should never compromise safety.

DEADLIFTS

The traditional deadlift is one of the most beneficial exercises you can do because it develops the hamstrings and spinal erectors as no other movement can. In terms of separating serious powerlifters from long-winded pretenders, the deadlift has an important advantage over the barbell squat: with deadlifts, you either pull the weight off the floor or you fail miserably.

With heavy squats, you can impress the uninitiated with what ultimately amounts to a treacherous good morning. We've all seen it happen. A novice lifter begins to descend in his first rep, the weight starts to feel extremely heavy, and all of a sudden his torso is parallel to the floor and his butt is somewhere near Idaho. He gives it all he has, somehow manages to return to the starting position, and goes crashing into the power rack.

Push presses, start.

Push presses, finish.

Deadlifts, start.

Deadlifts, finish.

Deadlifts, midrange.

The deadlift is less ambiguous; the bar must be pulled from the floor to the point at which the lifter is standing with shoulders back and legs straight. You can tell when lifters fail to lock their shoulders, and you can see them hitch the bar on their thighs when the weight is too heavy. In terms of execution, then, the deadlift is more straightforward. Performed consistently over a period of years, it offers something no other exercise can produce: a grip from hell.

As Franco Columbu wrote in his 1977 book *Winning Bodybuilding*, "This exercise will build you a grip that would make an oyster wince." And as those who follow bodybuilding know, few physique athletes could approach Franco in the deadlift. He was every bit as good a powerlifter as he was a bodybuilder, and aside from blowing up hot-water bottles, the deadlift was his forte.

Watch *Pumping Iron*, and you'll notice that when it came to muscle density, Franco and Arnold dominated their competition. Their backs were more complete than those of the other bodybuilders, and their lower backs, in particular, looked like bronzed Christmas trees. Franco and Arnold believed in big, basic exercises and performed countless sets of squats, bench presses, and deadlifts. You'll see a few cable movements in *Pumping Iron*, but for the most part, barbells and dumbbells led the charge. Bodybuilders had a different look and a different brand of strength in those days, and they generated much of that explosive strength by repeatedly pulling a loaded barbell off the floor.

When performing deadlifts, it's essential to keep your back as straight as possible, thereby reducing the amount of pressure on your spinal cord. Keeping your spinal erectors flexed and your back relatively flat puts your back in extension. That's the ideal for this exercise.

Anyone who has ever completed a set of heavy deadlifts, however, knows that it's very difficult to maintain perfect extension. Few athletes can pull hundreds of pounds off the floor and stay completely extended throughout the set, so you can expect a certain amount of flexion in your back. The remedy is to maintain proper flexion and avoid massive hunching from start to finish. Serious injuries can occur when athletes step up to the deadlift bar and attempt to move the entire weight with the back.

To avoid injury and still lift the heaviest poundage possible, concentrate on sitting back when you reach down, grab the bar, and begin the set. As with heavy squats, you should drive the weight from your heels—not the balls of your feet—and use the powerful spinal erectors to your advantage. If you have trouble there, it probably means that the strength in your legs is not quite as developed as the strength in your various back muscles. The cure is to perform heavy squats, as discussed earlier.

Picture yourself at the bottom of a squat, and then picture yourself at the start of a deadlift. When your thighs are parallel to the floor in the squat, with your knees directly above your feet, you must lift the weight using the powerful gluteus and quadriceps muscles. If you sit back as you begin a set of deadlifts,

you'll use that explosion to your advantage. Conversely, if your butt shoots up right away and you get up on the balls of your feet, you won't involve your legs as much as you should, and you'll risk injury.

When I compete in deadlift meets, I enjoy not only the competition but also the conversations I have with other lifters. For example, a conversation I had with a fellow competitor at a 1966 meet in North Carolina resulted in a new approach to building explosion off the ground.

The man explained that he commonly trained deadlifts while standing on 100-pound Olympic plates instead of the gym floor, thus forcing himself to move the weight an extra few inches with each repetition. I hadn't tried that before, but after watching him win my division with impressive technique and excellent overall strength, I gave it a shot. I'm glad I did because those extra few inches really increased the workload by forcing me to lower my entire body with every rep.

If you have difficulty at the start of a deadlift—or even if you don't—you'll definitely benefit from this modification. You don't have to do it every time, but once every few workouts will make a difference. Simply stand two or three inches higher than you normally would, and keep the bar at its original level. For safety purposes, I recommend using hard rubber mats instead of iron plates, and make sure to wear a good pair of leather tennis shoes. Or, if you have a pair of construction boots with rubber soles, wear them; the raised heels will further increase your range of motion. You should notice a major change in workload. I've performed heavy squats for more than a decade, and as a result, I can really snap the weight from the floor when I begin a deadlift. My problem area, or sticking point, is near the top of the pull, and I recently began to incorporate heavy partials using a standard power rack.

A friend of mine, Charlie Petrone, president of Petrone Speed & Strength in Knoxville, Tennessee, draws an analogy between the deadlift and the 40-yard dash. When Charlie trains athletes for speed, he breaks the major sprints into segments. In other words, his athletes don't run 40-yard dashes to improve their 40-yard-dash times. Instead, they work on four 10-yard segments and ultimately achieve a greater, or faster, whole. The same logic can be applied to the deadlift.

Before I began to incorporate heavy partials, I typically deadlifted about 550 pounds in competition. I could pull more weight off the floor but would slow down as I neared the finish position. So, instead of performing standard deadlifts only, I now train in the power rack with up to 700 pounds on the bar. The range of motion is much shorter—I work primarily from the third ring—but partials have really strengthened the area where I've had the most difficulty. At my latest meet, I pulled 575, and I have little doubt that 600-plus is on the way.

If you're interested in developing a strong deadlift, then break down the movement and think about it. What part of the exercise is the most difficult? If your butt shoots up before the weight leaves the floor, try working with your feet elevated, as I described. If you can blast the weight off the ground but then hit a sticking point, use the power rack. Think about exactly where the pause takes place. If you're about six feet tall and it occurs near your knees, try doing three or four sets at the second-ring level. If you slow down just as you're about to finish the lift, work the third ring.

Partials provide an excellent avenue for breaking past plateaus, and they also develop muscularity throughout the upper and lower back. Professional bodybuilders Michael Francois and Dorian Yates are two proponents of partials, and they both have exceptional back development.

As the saying goes, you have to lift big to get big, and whether you fancy yourself a bodybuilder, a powerlifter, or a basic weight lifter, the deadlift can help to improve both your strength and your shape.

ROWS

In terms of isolating the lats and teres muscles, dumbbell rows tend to be superior to their barbell counterparts because they allow for a greater stretch at the bottom and a more intense contraction at the top. As with many other exercises, one of the most common mistakes you can make on rows—dumbbell or barbell—is to use too much weight. If your back hunches during a set of rows, the weight is too heavy. Your spinal erectors become exhausted, and you begin to heave the weight up and down. Instead of squeezing your shoulder blades together and staying locked in position, you sling the weight with your arms and somehow make it through the set.

Seasoned rowers keep their spinal erectors flexed throughout a set, thus allowing the torso to remain relatively still. When your lower back isn't flexed, your torso wanders all over the place, and the designated muscles aren't worked as thoroughly as they would be with correct form.

Another common training mistake involves the point at which the barbell or dumbbell comes into contact with the body at the top of the exercise. Lifters sometimes pull the weight to the chest instead of the abdomen, where it belongs. You'll generate a much better contraction in your major back muscles if you concentrate on pulling the weight to your abs.

You'll also enhance the contraction by wearing wrist straps to help reduce the biceps involvement. Gripping the bar should not be the central task of an exercise, but that's what happens to many beginning weight lifters because their grip strength is not well developed. So, if you haven't done so already, get yourself a good pair of straps, and use them for most of your pull movements. You'll notice the difference in the amount of work your back muscles are doing relative to your biceps.

In addition, always keep your knees slightly bent to reduce the pressure on your joints, and make sure to keep your head aligned with your spine.

When you perform dumbbell rows, begin your set by locking your spinal erectors as you position yourself with your torso parallel to the floor and one leg on a utility bench. Holding your back straight, row the dumbbell to your abdomen. Don't allow your torso to twist during the exercise; if you do, it probably

Dumbbell rows, start.

Dumbbell rows, finish.

means that the dumbbell is too heavy for you to handle in a controlled manner. Allow the dumbbell to drift slightly forward at the bottom to enhance the pull, and then power through your next repetition.

MEDIUM-GRIP CHINS

While there are several exercises you can perform to build thickness in the major back muscles, only one creates a pair of broad, sweeping lats. Medium-grip chins are an athlete's exercise; only a small fraction of the people in a given gym can perform them, and even fewer can do them properly. Police departments often use chins to assess the torso strength of prospective officers, and well they should. The exercise requires tremendous physical strength and the ability to keep the body on one vertical plane from start to finish.

Wrist straps are also an important factor on this exercise. Used appropriately, straps can help to reduce the role of the biceps and allow for a more intense contraction in the lats and rhomboids. With a good pair of straps, your arms become hooks, and you can apply the effort you would have needed to grip the bar to working your upper back.

Attach the straps to the point at which the chinning bar begins to curve downward. Never go wider than that point, for it puts your shoulders in danger and inhibits your ability to pull your shoulder blades together as you move through each rep.

Contract your lats not only as you pull your body up but also as you lower it. Novice weight lifters sometimes avoid chins because they can manage only two or three reps per set. If you struggle with this exercise, don't give up on it. Do as many reps as you can for three sets, and then go directly to the pull-down machine and do four sets of eight. Each time you train your back, do your chins and then challenge yourself to use more weight on the pull-down machine. Just don't challenge yourself to the point where your lower back becomes a hinge to sling the weight.

For advanced lifters, here's a new twist to the standard: Instead of letting your legs stay relatively involved during the exercise, extend them and hold them out in front of you during the set. If you've got the strength to perform strict chins, doing them that way enables you to increase the work on your lower abs and back. Picture yourself as a champion gymnast, moving strictly through each rep, totally under control. That's strength.

THE PROCESS OF WEIGHT LIFTING

Generally speaking, serious weight lifting is for serious people. Not everyone has the passion it takes to become successful, as gains come slowly after a few years on the job. You may add only 15 pounds to your maximum bench press over 12 months of lifting, but you can bet that those 15 pounds will require more effort than you had previously expended.

The people who become successful weight lifters are those who simply love it. They can't wait to get to the gym each day, but by the same token, they know that success in life requires a great deal more than the ability to pump heavy iron. They do other things and have other commitments, which is precisely the reason they excel. Few people become successful without some degree of balance. The burnout factor is just too great. So, strive to balance your lifting with professional endeavors, social functions, and personal relationships, and you'll be amazed at how well everything comes together to produce a greater whole.

As always, concentrate on the training poundages that you can handle safely. You are, after all, in pursuit of personal excellence, and you'll reach that point only by focusing on the task at hand and training to the best of your own ability.

A four-week program similar to the one I've used for about 12 years follows. Adjust your training poundages based on the number of reps required for each set. Remember to get a good stretch in before you handle a heavy weight, and never compromise your technique.

Pushdowns, start.

Pushdowns, finish.

Overhead extensions, start.

Overhead extensions, finish.

FOUR-WEEK POWER ROUTINE

Week 1
Day 1

Bench presses	$1 \times 8 \times 135$
	$1 \times 6 \times 225$
	$4 \times 5 \times 275$
Flat-bench dumbbell presses	$4 \times 8 \times 130s$
Parallel bar dips	$4 \times 12\text{--}15$

Day 2

Squats	$1 \times 8 \times 135$
	$1 \times 6 \times 225$
	$1 \times 6 \times 315$
	$4 \times 6 \times 405$
Sissy squats	$4 \times 10\text{--}12$
Standing calf raises	4×12

Day 3: Off

Day 4

Medium-grip chins	$6 \times 10\text{--}12$
Dumbbell rows	$4 \times 8 \times 130s$
Close-grip chins	$4 \times 10\text{--}12$

Day 5

Incline barbell presses	$1 \times 8 \times 135$
	$1 \times 6 \times 185$
	$4 \times 6 \times 225$
Flat-bench dumbbell presses	$4 \times 8 \times 130s$
Parallel bar dips	$4 \times 12\text{--}15$

Day 6

Deadlifts	$1 \times 6 \times 135$
	$1 \times 6 \times 225$
	$1 \times 4 \times 315$
	$1 \times 4 \times 405$
	$3 \times 3 \times 505$
Medium-grip chins	$5 \times 10\text{--}12$

Day 7: Off

Week 2
Day 1

Bench presses	$1 \times 8 \times 135$
	$1 \times 6 \times 225$
	$4 \times 4 \times 285$
Flat-bench dumbbell presses	$4 \times 6 \times 140s$
Parallel bar dips	$4 \times 12\text{--}15$

Day 2

Squats	$1 \times 8 \times 135$
	$1 \times 6 \times 225$
	$1 \times 6 \times 315$
	$4 \times 5 \times 425$
Sissy squats	$4 \times 10\text{--}12$
Standing calf raises	4×12

Day 3: Off

Day 4

Medium-grip chins	$6 \times 10\text{--}12$
Bent-over barbell rows	$1 \times 8 \times 135$
	$4 \times 8 \times 225$
Close-grip chins	$4 \times 10\text{--}12$

Day 5

Incline barbell presses	$1 \times 8 \times 135$
	$1 \times 6 \times 185$
	$4 \times 5 \times 235$
Flat-bench dumbbell presses	$4 \times 8 \times 130s$
Parallel bar dips	$4 \times 12\text{--}15$

Day 6

Deadlifts	$1 \times 6 \times 135$
	$1 \times 6 \times 225$
	$1 \times 4 \times 315$
	$1 \times 4 \times 405$
	$3 \times 2 \times 525$
Medium-grip chins	$5 \times 10\text{--}12$

Day 7: Off

Week 3
Day 1

Bench presses	$1 \times 8 \times 135$
	$1 \times 6 \times 225$
	$4 \times 3 \times 300$
Flat-bench dumbbell presses	$2 \times 6 \times 140s$
	$2 \times 4 \times 150s$
Parallel bar dips	$4 \times 12\text{--}15$

Day 2

Squats	$1 \times 8 \times 135$
	$1 \times 6 \times 225$
	$1 \times 6 \times 315$
	$4 \times 4 \times 455$
Dumbbell squats	$3 \times 10\text{--}12$
Seated calf raises	4×12

Day 3: Off

Day 4

Medium-grip chins	6 × 10–12
Dumbbell rows	4 × 4 × 140s
Close-grip chins	4 × 10–12

Day 5

Incline barbell presses	1 × 8 × 135
	1 × 6 × 185
	4 × 4 × 250
Flat-bench dumbbell presses	4 × 6 × 140s
Parallel bar dips	4 × 12–15

Day 6

Deadlifts	1 × 6 × 135
	1 × 6 × 225
	1 × 4 × 315
	1 × 4 × 405
	1 × 2 × 495
	2 × 1 × 550
Medium-grip chins	5 × 10–12

Day 7: Off

Week 4
Day 1

Bench presses	1 × 8 × 135
	1 × 6 × 225
	4 × 3 × 310
Flat-bench dumbbell presses	4 × 4 × 150s
Parallel bar dips	4 × 12–15

Day 2

Squats	1 × 8 × 135
	1 × 6 × 225
	1 × 6 × 315
	4 × 3 × 475
Lunges (per leg)	3 × 6 × 225
Seated calf raises	4 × 12

Day 3: Off

Day 4

Medium-grip chins	6 × 10–12
Bent-over barbell rows	1 × 8 × 135
	1 × 6 × 225
	3 × 6 × 250
Close-grip chins	4 × 10–12

Day 5

Incline barbell presses	1 × 8 × 135
	1 × 6 × 185
	4 × 3 × 260
Flat-bench dumbbell presses	4 × 7 × 140s
Parallel bar dips	4 × 12–15

Day 6

Deadlifts	1 × 6 × 135
	1 × 6 × 225
	1 × 4 × 315
	1 × 4 × 405
	1 × 2 × 495
	1 × 1 × 550
	1 × 1 × 575
Medium-grip chins	5 × 10–12

Day 7: Off

Chapter 15

MONSTER PUMP
TIPS FOR OUTRAGEOUS MUSCLE GROWTH

BY C. S. SLOAN

Bodybuilders have always considered the pump to be a measure of a proper workout. While it doesn't guarantee muscle growth, it's a pretty good way of gauging whether a muscle is responding well or whether you're overtrained. You know you're on the right track when your muscle blows up after only a few sets, but when you're overtrained, the pump becomes more elusive than ever. Old-time lifters such as Steve Reeves, Reg Park, John Grimek, and Larry Scott understood the importance of pumping a muscle, or flushing, as it's sometimes called. They knew that a muscle that pumps up easily is more likely to grow than one that doesn't.

It was nothing for the bodybuilders of the 1950s and '60s to do 50 sets of bench presses or barbell curls. They just did whatever it took to get their biceps swollen like balloons. Of course, they didn't take each set to the psycho level that many of today's champs do, but they nonetheless knew the power of the pump. Park, for example, performed only one exercise for his arms, but he did it until his muscle was red from the engorged blood. Using a

weight that allowed him to get 6 to 10 reps, he performed as many sets as it took until he achieved a massive pump.

Grimek, to this day, recommends that you not count sets, but instead train a muscle until it's fully congested. (He calls it the congestive principle.) Once the target muscle is pumped to its fullest degree, there's no reason to continue with more sets. That only leads to overtraining.

The great Serge Nubret was always searching for the ultimate pump. It was his goal every time he entered the gym. Like Park, he often performed a single exercise until his muscles were pumped to their fullest. Nubret liked to keep his reps high, often doing 20 sets of 20 reps on wide-grip bench presses. There's no way you can't pump your muscles to the max with that technique.

Another living example of the importance of the pump is three-time Mr. Olympia Sergio Oliva. When Oliva first got into bodybuilding, he was under the tutelage of one Bob Gajda, a proponent of a system known as Peripheral Heart Action, or PHA. Gajda's system is very

similar to circuit training in that you do one exercise for one muscle group, immediately followed by another exercise for a different muscle group. You take no rest between exercises until you finish working your entire body in one circuit. The main problem with this type of exercise regimen is that you don't keep the blood flow localized in one area and you can't devote your complete attention to a single muscle group. You're just too worried about completing the circuit.

Oliva actually did make pretty good gains using this system—probably due to his phenomenal genetics—but it wasn't until he started using a routine that allowed him to really blast each bodypart and get a good pump that he realized his full potential in the sport. Oliva's favorite way to work out was with high sets and lots of reps. He often employed a form of rest/pause training, in which, for example, if he was working his chest, he'd do a set of bench presses for six to eight reps, pause for a few breaths, perform another set, pause for a few more breaths, crank out another set, and so on. That type

of fast, localized training gave Oliva a tremendous pump and helped him build one of the most amazing physiques ever.

Probably the best reason to strive for a great pump in your training can be summed up in two words: Arnold Schwarzenegger. Arnold would never have thought of leaving the gym if his muscles weren't blown up to the max. He, too, believed in high sets and high reps, and he also espoused hitting the target bodypart from every angle. That type of training brought him fantastic pumps and incredible development.

Not that the pump isn't the Holy Grail for today's bodybuilding stars as well. Flex Wheeler, Paul Dillett, Kevin Levrone, Nasser El Sonbaty, Vince Taylor, Shawn Ray, and most of the other current pros use the pump to assess how well their training is going.

Porter Cottrell has said that he determines when to quit his workout by how good his pump is. Like Grimek before him, he works a muscle until it's congested and then, but only then, stops. He may discover right in the middle of a set that he cannot pump up a muscle

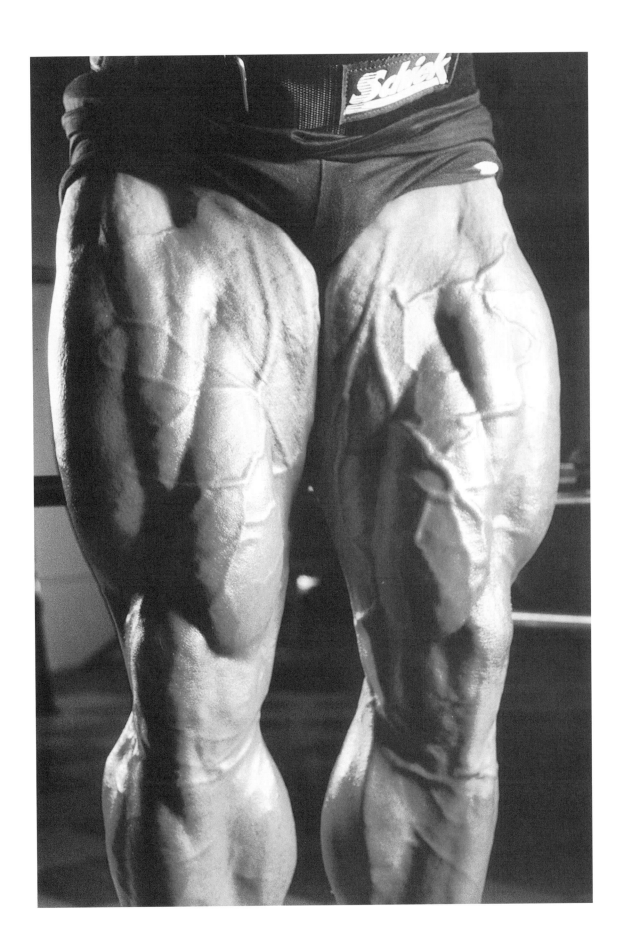

TRAINING

There are many things you can do to improve your pump. Bodybuilders of the past tended to perform a lot of sets. While this is one technique you can use, it's probably not the best. Doing a lot of sets tends to lead to overtraining. The real key to getting a good growth pump is to do the most work in the shortest amount of time possible. Let's look at some techniques that can help you do this.

High reps

This is a favorite pumping method of bodybuilders past and present—and probably those of the future. That includes Scott, Schwarzenegger, Oliva, Nubret, and Dave Draper. If you have a muscle group that just

anymore. When that happens, he stops the set cold, realizing that his muscles are pumped to their fullest.

That's how some of the most famous bodybuilders past and present have trained for the pump. The question is, What's the best way for you to do it? There are several variables. Your training, diet, and supplements have an effect on the quality of the pump you get at every workout.

strings, and calves, give it a try. I'm talking about the 35-to-50 range for your upper legs and maybe even more for your calves.

Reg Park, who had an astounding pair of calves, always trained his lower legs with incredibly high reps. Fifty was probably the minimum. He also believed in performing full reps and making sure to get a deep stretch at the bottom. Try a few sets of 50 to 100 reps on your calf exercises, and prepare yourself for the pump. Just make sure you don't perform bouncy, herky-jerky reps. Do as Park did and get a deep, full stretch followed by a hard contraction at the top.

Minimum rest between sets

Larry Scott calls it "racing the pump." It goes back to the idea of doing the greatest amount of work in the shortest possible time. The best way to race the pump is to take no more than a minute's rest between sets. Thirty seconds is even better. Make sure your reps never creep below six. Of course, you won't be able to use as much weight, and you may have to decrease the weight with each subsequent set, but the intensity factor stays high, which brings some great muscle growth.

isn't responding well to heavy weights and you're having a hard time pumping it, unleash some high reps on it for a month or so, and see what happens. Besides ensuring a needed growth pump, high reps help to build up the capillaries and neuromuscular pathways in a muscle. That will help the muscle respond better to heavier weights when you switch back.

The lower body in particular seems to respond well to high-rep training. When you really want a good pump in your quads, ham-

There are several other exercises that work well with down-the-racks. Dumbbell bench presses (flat-bench, incline, or decline), bent-over laterals, flye movements, lying triceps extensions, and curls all work well. Just remember to take absolutely no rest between sets as you move down the rack, and don't take more than a minute after each series—or more than the time it takes your training partner to finish his or her set.

Frank Zane is another bodybuilder who in his prime had some of the best delts in the business. They were full, round, and symmetrical and really complemented the rest of his physique. Zane went for the pump in his delt workouts, and trisets were his intensity technique of choice.

Intensity techniques

There are several fantastic intensity techniques you can use to pump a muscle. Early in his training career, Scott didn't have the widest shoulders—but he knew what to do about it. Besides changing the way he did certain shoulder movements, he incorporated what I like to call "up and down the rack" sets. These are similar to drop sets.

For instance, on dumbbell presses, he'd start with the 60-pounders and work up to the 80s, making sure to get six to eight reps on each set. Scott then took a brief rest and started working his way down the rack until he made it back to the 60-pound dumbbells. He then followed this torture with up-and-down-the-rack lateral raises. Scott definitely knew how to race the pump.

Spider curls.

He'd grab a pair of moderately heavy dumbbells and start with lateral raises. When he reached failure, he'd do a set of front raises without putting the dumbbells down, front raises being easier than laterals. After hitting muscular failure on the front raises, he'd continue without rest with a set of upright rows for his rear delts. Try this in your shoulder workouts for a better, faster pump.

You can also perform trisets by arranging three exercises relatively close together and doing one immediately after the other. Here are some great trisets: straight-arm pull-downs, chin-ups, and low-cable rows for back; incline bench presses, dumbbell bench presses, and dumbbell flyes for chest; dumbbell curls, incline dumbbell curls, and concentration curls for biceps; pushdowns, overhead extensions, and bench dips for triceps; leg presses, sissy squats, and leg extensions for quads; stiff-legged deadlifts, lying leg curls, and standing alternate leg curls for hamstrings; and seated calf raises, leg-press calf raises, and standing machine raises for calves.

If you're fairly new to the iron game and find that trisets are a little too much for you to handle, try some supersets instead.

Another great intensity technique is burns. You probably won't find too many trainees performing burns in the average gym, and that's too bad because they are terrific and can really provide that extra edge for an even better pump. Burns are little half or quarter reps done at the end of a set of full reps in order to continue the set and increase the intensity. The technique was popularized back in the late '50s but somehow got lost in all the training trends that have come and gone in recent years. Maybe a little revision is in order.

NUTRITION

No matter how good your training program is, you'll never get the type of outrageous pumps it takes to build a great physique unless your eating habits are solidly in the right place. Twinkies, soft drinks, and potato chips just won't cut it. The first thing your diet needs is carbohydrates. You'll never attain a decent pump without enough glycogen loaded in the muscles. The only way your muscles store glycogen is through the intake of carbs.

One of the more popular diets of late is a high-fat, high-protein, low-carb regimen. This diet is nothing new. A lot of the bodybuilders of the past used it. It's also a favorite of the Iron Guru, Vince Gironda, who's been touting

the benefits of that type of eating for years. He knows a lot about it and says its main downfall is that the muscles don't store glycogen properly.

Some people do find such a diet beneficial, however. If you're going to use it, make sure you go off it on the weekends and load up on plenty of carbs, as Gironda recommends.

SUPPLEMENTS

There are other dietary factors you can control that affect the training pump. Supplements are the key here. A number of products on the market are said to be good for creating a more dramatic pump. Their effectiveness ranges from so-so to great.

MCT

Medium-chain triglyceride, or MCT, oil is one of the best supplements you can use. Your body tends to use it for energy, allowing your muscles to store more glycogen, which, in turn, brings you a better pump.

Vanadyl sulfate

Vanadyl sulfate is another supplement that works well, at least for some trainees. Of the people I know who have tried it, half rave about vanadyl sulfate and the other half say they didn't notice much difference. Nonetheless, you should give it a try. If it works for you, you'll feel the effects after only a couple of days. Your muscles will look fuller, and your pumps will be more intense.

Inosine

Inosine is also a substance that gets mixed reviews; however, the majority of bodybuilders feel they can honestly tell a difference in their pumps when they're on it. Supposedly, the effect is due to increased ATP stores. Your best bet is to buy a small bottle and decide for yourself.

Mahuang

The herb mahuang can really help bring an extra something to your pumps—for the simple reason that it enhances your intensity level quite a bit. (As you should know by now, workout intensity is the main criterion for an overwhelming pump.) If you've never used mahuang before, be careful you don't take too much. The side effects can include dizziness and lack of appetite.

The four supplements discussed here are the ones most often used for improving the training pump. There are many other good supplements around, but it's debatable whether they have any effect for this purpose. These include creatine monohydrate, niacin, chromium picolinate, glutamine, and ornithine alpha-ketoglutarate.

Just remember that no matter how many supplements you take, you'll never get a good pump if your diet is not on target. Eat well first, and supplement second. No one ever built a fantastic physique by doing it backward.

So, there you have it: a blueprint for increasing the intensity of your pump. Use these tips on a regular basis, and your physique will soar to new levels.

The really great bodybuilders, such as Larry Scott, Sergio Oliva, Frank Zane, and Arnold Schwarzenegger (seen here), developed the power of concentration to a very high level.

Chapter 16

VINCE GIRONDA'S TRAINING SECRETS

BY VINCE GIRONDA

I think that rules are made to be challenged, questioned, changed, or broken completely. There is no absolutely right or wrong way to work out. Too many bodybuilders slave away year in and year out using exercises and concepts that they never bother to analyze.

When I experiment with a new exercise, I don't do it for a week or two and expect to feel or see any difference. I give it a chance and let it become a habit. Any exercise I recommend is one that I personally tried and tested for at least nine months. That way, you can benefit from a proven result.

I'm flexible in my thinking, and I give new concepts a fair and working chance. I have no magical secrets other than keeping an open mind. If the old, worn patterns fail to produce, throw them out. If they're partially successful, creatively improve them. If an old routine or exercise combination works, I'll use it. Why tinker with a good thing? If I get the results I want in changing, developing, and renewing my body, then I've found a road map to the perfection I seek.

Most of my pupils arrived at my gym underweight and lacking muscle size. If someone needed to gain 20, 30, 40, or 50 pounds to reach his goals, I gave him the information presented here, along with the admonition that he strive to gain only quality muscle mass—in the right places. In other words, he should work to improve the shape and symmetry of his body by adding mass to his weak points.

Larry Scott came to me weighing 157 pounds. When he won his final Mr. Olympia title, he weighed 207. Larry did it the right way. He gained quality muscle and reshaped his physique by working his weak points harder than his strong points. To compensate for his narrow clavicle, he built massive delts and arms. Take heed of Scott's success: gain all the weight and muscle you need to reach your goals, but only in the right places.

Larry Scott is just one of the many hundreds who have used my weight-gaining procedures. Gene Mozée came to me when he was about 18 and told me he wanted to weigh 200

WEIGHT-GAINING PROCEDURES

Blood builds muscle. Taking 10 desiccated-liver tablets and one high-potency B-complex tablet every three hours produces a high red blood cell count and more blood volume. Iron also is an oxygen carrier, as is wheat-germ oil. Those who want to gain weight should substitute certified raw milk for coffee, too.

Observe the following rules:

1. Never overeat. Instead, eat smaller meals every three hours. That way, nutrients are available all day long for energy and building and repairing muscle tissue.
2. Never let yourself go hungry. Don't skip a scheduled meal. Keep your body constantly supplied with the fuel it needs to meet the demands of your exercise program and work.
3. Absolutely no smoking. Nicotine constricts the capillaries for as long as eight hours, as well as burning 25 milligrams of vitamin C per cigarette.
4. Control your emotions—don't let them control you. Calm down. Slow down. When you're too tense and too active, you're constantly in a catabolic state.
5. Be sure to sit or lie down with your feet and legs elevated after every meal. That lets the blood in the body concentrate around the stomach for maximum digestion.
6. Stay focused. Keep your eye on the prize. Don't waste energy playing football, softball, or other vigorous recreational sports. Those activities will hinder muscle growth and weight gain.

Here are a few other useful suggestions. A European weight-gaining trick that really works is to drink equal parts cream and ginger ale. Drink this as a between-meals pickup at 10, 2, and 4 o'clock. I've seen students gain as much as 40 pounds using this. It works very well for football players who need more weight and size to be competitive.

pounds—he was 150 at the time. I didn't recognize him when he returned a couple of years later weighing 220 and with 20-inch arms. He said it was the weight-gaining information I gave him that enabled him to build such muscle mass. The following is the information I gave all my underweight pupils.

Stay focused.

It's important to keep a regular schedule for eating and sleeping as well for working out. Eat at the same time, train at the same time, and relax and retire at the same time every day. The body responds best to routine.

Don't stuff yourself with three giant meals a day! Your body won't use the food efficiently. The question is, Why do you feel the need for more food than the body actually requires? The answer lies in what you eat. The body interprets food as nutrients, vital minerals, vitamins, and enzymes. If the food you eat doesn't contain sufficient amounts of those elements, you're bound to overeat in order to feel satisfied.

To build a fabulous physique, you must also consider the mental state. The masters of Zen, hatha yoga, and judo teach us that human beings have lost touch with the instinctive wisdom of the body. I'm not sure they're entirely right. I've seen many top bodybuilders who seem to have this instinctive wisdom. The point, however, is well taken. It's important to be in touch with this source.

To obtain this state of awareness, the Zen masters advise us to be completely aware of

what we are doing at the moment. Physical discipline should be free of all craving for becoming. One should see and feel as if one had already obtained the desired state of being. In other words, you need to concentrate: to bring all of your powers, faculties, or activities to bear on a course of action or thought.

It's been my observation that the really great bodybuilders, such as Larry Scott, Sergio Oliva, Frank Zane, and Arnold Schwarzenegger, among those who trained at my gym, developed this power of concentration to a very high level. They always kept totally focused on what they were doing and where they were going. They visualized themselves as having already won their Mr. Olympia titles and fully developed their potentials long before they actually achieved that. You would do well to emulate these champions.

Bill Pearl.

Chapter 17

BILL PEARL'S SECRETS FOR BUILDING MASSIVE SIZE AND POWER

BY BILL PEARL AS TOLD TO GENE MOZÉE

Bill Pearl stands as a colossus in the world of bodybuilding. From the time he won the Mr. America title in 1953 until he won the Mr. Universe pro title in 1971, he remained in near-peak condition. No other bodybuilder has come close to remaining at the top for that long. He went out a champion of champions, having beaten Sergio Oliva, Frank Zane, Dave Draper, Franco Columbu, Serge Nubret, and Reg Park. Perhaps even more astonishing, he weighed 40 pounds more at the Pro Universe than he had at the Mr. America—with more cuts. In 1971, he was the heaviest, at 242 pounds, and the oldest, at 41, man to ever win the National Amateur Bodybuilders Association (NABBA) Mr. Universe.

Remember, this was before anabolic steroids ruled the competitive bodybuilding world. Bill was the first to sport more than 230 pounds of hard, muscular mass, and he did it without human growth hormone supplements or any of the other sophisticated drugs that are producing the mass monsters in vogue today. Not only that, but he was on a totally vegetarian diet.

Bill has trained thousands of people at his gyms over the years. He estimates that more than 90 percent of the training queries he has received have to do with building mass. The following advice from Bill Pearl is designed for the average bodybuilder who wants to get bigger and stronger as quickly as possible.

Muscle mass is generally associated with power. A big man is considered a strong man—if he has the right kind of weight. For some people, of course, mass is an asset regardless of shape—sumo wrestlers, football linemen, shot-putters. For bodybuilders, however, the object is to build muscle mass without fat.

The following workout routines are designed to increase muscle mass throughout your body and to lay the foundation for developing a complete physique, one without weak points.

If you want to gain 25 or more pounds of muscle, start by doing Program 1 and work up to Program 2, regardless of how long you've been training. It may be a lot less than you've been doing, but it will give your body a chance to rebuild and prepare your ligaments and

tendons for the stress that will be placed on them later. It's important to do these exercises in the exact order presented. You must get a full extension and contraction on every rep. Use lighter weights at first—about two-thirds of your maximum—so that you can do the recommended number of reps.

Don't hurry through your sets. Rest for about three minutes between sets. This pace will let you use heavier weights as your stamina improves. Your recuperative power is the true measure of the pace you should maintain. Because of the long rest periods between sets, I suggest that you wear a sweatshirt to keep from cooling off too much.

Keep an accurate record of your training. Record your bodyweight and measurements before you begin this program, and remeasure every six weeks. If after several weeks you haven't gained weight, experiment with your calories. Don't expect a big increase in weight in the first week or two because your system must adjust to the increased workload and expenditure of energy.

TRAINING HINTS

It's very important to breathe correctly when training for mass and power. Do not hold your breath during the hardest part of a lift. Remember to exhale.

Start with a light weight on each exercise, about two-thirds of your maximum. When you can easily do two more reps than the recommended number, add poundage. Keep trying to increase the weight on all exercises as long you can do them with correct form. Always do a full extension and contraction on each rep.

Program 3 focuses on heavy weights. Start with a warm-up set and then use poundages that force you to work very hard. You'll need more rest between sets, but three to five minutes should be adequate.

Sleep and relaxation are very important. While some people may need more sleep and some need less, plan to get at least eight hours of sound sleep. Going to bed at the same time

every night helps the body to regulate itself and produce faster muscle growth.

A proper attitude plays a large role in building size and strength. Think positively about all of your daily activities, not just your gym work. A healthy, positive attitude will improve your body and make you a better person.

Eat a good breakfast. You'll give your body the fuel it needs to operate efficiently. Start the day with at least 50 grams of protein, plus some fats and carbohydrates.

Eat at regular times and intervals. If you find that three meals a day doesn't provide enough calories to add muscle size, eat smaller meals—one about every three hours. If you're very underweight, you can make outstanding gains by drinking a quart of milk during your workouts.

If your goal is rapid weight and muscle gain, you need 4,000 to 5,000 calories a day and 150 grams of protein. Try to get most of the protein from food rather than from supplements. A good protein drink or two is useful but shouldn't replace your regular meals. You should also take vitamins B, C, and E with your meals.

DIET

It's difficult to recommend a diet that works for everyone. People have differing tastes and finances, and the availability of foods varies from area to area and season to season. Some people are allergic to certain foods. You must choose the foods that work for you, but there are some general guidelines that apply to virtually everyone:

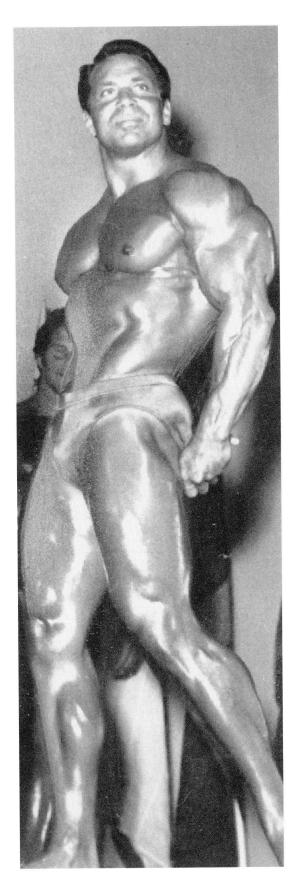

The great English philosopher John Locke wrote, "We are born with faculties and powers capable of almost anything, such as at least would carry us further than can be easily imagined; but it is only the exercise of those powers which gives us ability and skill in anything, and leads us towards perfection." By using your faculties and powers, you can have a more massive and powerful physique. These basic programs provide a proven route to physical perfection.

THE ROUTINES

Program 1*

Dumbbell swings	1 × 10
Bent-knee leg raises	1 × 30
Good mornings	1 × 10
Breathing squats**	2 × 15
Bent-arm lateral raises**	2 × 12
Calf raises	3 × 20
Shrugs	2 × 8
Bench presses	2 × 8
Rows	2 × 8
Behind-the-neck presses	2 × 8
Curls	2 × 8
Bent-legged deadlifts	3 × 5

*Do this workout three times a week with a day of rest between workouts, and follow the program for six weeks.

**Alternate sets on the squats and laterals.

Program 2*

Dumbbell swings	1 × 10–15
Bent-knee sit-ups	1 × 15–20
Dumbbell side bends	1 × 15–20
Alternate leg raises	1 × 10–30
Parallel squats	3–5 × 6–8
Bent-arm pull-overs	3–5 × 8–10
Calf raises	3 × 15–20
Upright rows	2 × 8
Military presses	2 × 5–6
One-arm rows	3 × 8
Bent-legged deadlifts	2 × 8
Incline dumbbell presses	2 × 6–8
Bent-arm lateral raises	2 × 6–8
Dumbbell triceps extensions	3 × 6–8
Standing dumbbell curls	3 × 6–8

*Follow this routine three days a week for six weeks.

Program 3*

Bent-knee sit-ups	1 × 25
Bent-leg raises	2 × 25
Bench presses	5 × 5
Behind-the-neck presses	5 × 5
Pulldowns to the front	5 × 5
Barbell rows	3 × 6
Barbell curls	4 × 6
Barbell triceps extensions	4 × 6
Bench squats	5 × 5

*Follow this routine three days a week for six weeks.

In 1971, Bill Pearl won the NABBA Mr. Universe pro title, and a new guy named Arnold won the amateur title.

Chapter 18

SERGIO OLIVA'S SATURATION BOMBING ARM ROUTINE

BY SERGIO OLIVA AS TOLD TO GENE MOZÉE

Sergio Oliva is a bodybuilding phenomenon. He was the first muscular giant to appear on the scene with incredible size and laser-sharp definition—and legitimate 21-inch arms. In 1967, he gave the bodybuilding world a historic 21-gun salute while winning his first Mr. Olympia title. The legendary Bill Pearl said, "Sergio was ahead of his time. That thin-skinned, vascular, highly defined look wasn't in vogue until Sergio arrived." That's probably because no one had ever before reached Oliva's level of massive, striated muscularity combined with near-perfect proportions.

I've seen many bodybuilders who had sensational arm development. Back in the 1950s, there were the fabulous arms of Marvin Eder, Bob Shealy, Joe Sanceri, Babe Stansbury, Steve Reeves, Clancy Ross, Jack Delinger, Malcomb Brenner, and Reg Park. All of those stars had arms that measured 18 to 19 inches in peak contest shape.

In the early- to mid-1960s, Freddy Ortiz ($19^1/2$ inches), Larry Scott ($20^1/4$), Dave Draper ($20^1/2$), and Bill Pearl ($20^1/2$) were the reigning kings of arm size and muscularity, but in 1967,

Sergio Oliva topped them all when his fabulous guns extended the tape measure to a full $21^1/2$ inches. Not only were his arms huge, but they were also ripped to shreds with dazzling definition and deeply chiseled separation. His arms were totally developed from the deltoid to the elbow. They were wide, full, and thick from every angle. In fact, I've never seen anyone whose arms were as impressive as Sergio's were when they were hanging at his sides relaxed. His triceps development was arguably the greatest ever.

Remember that Sergio reached this milestone in bodybuilding history before the arrival of human growth hormone and the sophisticated injectable steroids that are available to modern muscle stars. It's a good thing, too, in my opinion. Sergio and the other superstars mentioned did it with hard work and good nutrition.

Look at the champions of the past who continued to compete or give posing exhibitions for 20 or more years—Pearl, Park, Scott, Serge Nubret, Lou Ferrigno, Albert Beckles, Frank Zane, and Robby Robinson. Sergio—a

study in bodybuilding longevity—has been at the top, or nearly so, for 30 years! Today's champs seldom last longer than 10 years. Steroid burnout? I think it's more than a possibility.

During the many opportunities I had to observe Sergio train at the legendary Vince's Gym in Studio City, California, when he was visiting the West Coast for posing exhibitions, I was able to gain valuable insight into his training methods. His concentration was so intense that he never spoke to anyone during his workout, except maybe a few words to Vince Gironda. After he finished working out, however, he was quite gregarious and displayed a great sense of humor. He would answer questions about his training thoroughly. One time, he described the program that built those 21-inch-plus arms.

"The Myth."

Sergio's arms were totally developed from the deltoid to the elbow.

SUPERSETS AND SUPERCONCENTRATION

When Sergio began training in his native Cuba in 1960, his arms were only 13 inches. At that time, he was an Olympic weight lifter and did only exercises that would build strength for that sport. Even so, his arms grew rapidly and were 17 inches when he reached a bodyweight of 198 pounds.

After defecting to the United States in 1962 and eventually settling in Chicago, he began bodybuilding at the Duncan YMCA. Although his arms were large and full, they were not very shapely, lacking a good biceps peak and sweeping triceps. He also needed sharp separation between the individual muscles and much greater definition.

"Size alone is not everything," explained Sergio. "When I won the Junior Mr. America title in 1966, I had built my arms up to 19 inches. My arm size increased to 20 by the time I won the Mr. World contest. But when I say that arm size isn't everything, here is a perfect example. In my first try for the Mr. Olympia crown, I was defeated, and I am sure that incomplete arm development—regardless of how massive my arms were—cost me the title."

Sergio was criticized at the time because his physique lacked separation, even though he was in top shape, without an ounce of fat. "So unanimous was the criticism that I had to completely reassess my development," he said. "It was then that I realized I had to discard all the training techniques I had been using and find new ones that would be more effective."

He started studying all the training methods of the champions and reading everything he could find on arm training, seeking the answer to the problem of increasing shape and definition. He eventually incorporated many of those ideas into his own unique system.

"Most bodybuilders think that just the biceps and triceps form the total upper arm," Sergio stated. "Not true—the brachialis underlies the biceps and inserts near the elbow. This muscle is essential, for without its full development, the elbow area looks weak and underdeveloped."

Sergio explained that the brachialis is brought into use during curling and reverse curling movements. "It can be especially developed by the reverse curl—an exercise that I have always included in my workouts. Look at any of my arm poses, and you can clearly see the brachialis development.

"You should consider the upper arms as being composed of three muscles—the biceps, triceps, and brachialis," Sergio continued, "and each must be fully developed if you want the

"I am convinced that without concentration, you can't develop a championship physique."

pump and forces them to grow larger and more defined more rapidly," he emphasized.

Sergio considers concentration to be the "true key to success in bodybuilding." He said, "I am convinced that without concentration, you can't develop a championship physique." He added that without concentration, your physique will be incomplete and not symmetrical. "Therefore, I work hard and force every rep of every set, all the while concentrating to the limit of my capability. I keep my mind focused directly on the actual movement of the weight—on the exact muscle being worked and on the correctness of my form."

Sergio credits the combination of supersets and maximum concentration with adding the size, shape, and separation that enabled him to win the Mr. Olympia title in 1967. "I can't stress the importance of concentration too much," he said. "Keep a constant reminder in your gym or locker with a sign that says 'Concentrate.' If you're preoccupied with other things, your workout will be largely wasted. And talk *after* your workout—not during it."

acme of arm development. That is how I got my arms up to 21½ inches."

Sergio used two particular techniques to the fullest to blast his arms past the 21-inch barrier: supersets and superconcentration. It's one thing to perform supersets—quite another to perform them with the utmost concentration. He favored supersets because they are a time-saver that enabled him to get more into—and out of—his workouts. "They make it possible to attack my arms more fiercely, giving them a saturation blitz that brings an ultimate

Sergio trains his arms twice a week, on Tuesday and Saturday. Other than a warm-up superset for the abdominals, he devotes the entire workout to his arms. Here's the routine. It takes him about two hours and is made up of just five supersets.

SERGIO OLIVA'S SATURATION BOMBING ARM ROUTINE

Superset 1: For mass

Standing barbell curls	5 × 8
Reverse barbell curls	5 × 15

Superset 2: For full development

Scott curls on machine*	5 × 8
Standing barbell extensions	5 × 8

Superset 3: For mass and power

Lying barbell extensions	5 × 8
Standing dumbbell extensions	5 × 8

Superset 4: For biceps shape and cuts

Seated dumbbell curls	5 × 8–10
Dumbbell concentration curls	5 × 10

Superset 5: Finishing triceps pumper

Press-downs	5 × 10
Reverse press-downs	5 × 10

*Sergio used the Scott curl machine at the Duncan YMCA, rather than the usual Scott curl bench, but you can get the same terrific benefit with either piece of equipment.

SERGIO'S ARM-TRAINING TIPS

1. This program is only for very advanced veteran bodybuilders, and even they should break into it gradually. It's definitely not for beginning or intermediate trainees.
2. Use strict form on all exercises so that the target muscle gets the total benefit of the movement. Keep your body movement to a minimum at all times.
3. If you're really advanced in arm work, don't stop after five complete supersets of the Scott curls–and–standing extensions combo, Superset 2. Instead, decrease the weight on both exercises by 20 pounds and do three supersets, increasing the reps to 10. Also, do them a bit faster than the first five supersets. This saturation blitz really pumps the arms to the maximum.
4. Handle as heavy a weight as possible on all exercises, but don't sacrifice form for poundage. Always strive for a complete range of motion on every movement.
5. For Superset 4, keep your body perfectly still on both exercises and use

very strict form. Concentrate intensely on the action of the biceps, and cramp and tense them at the top of the curling movement.

6. On the press-downs, always make sure that your body is solidly planted, that only the triceps work, and that you apply equal pressure with both arms.

7. Superset 5, the finishing triceps pumper, not only ensures you of a massive pump, but it guarantees complete development as well.

8. If you want maximum gains, concentrate on every rep of every set of every exercise.

9. Make sure you get lots of rest and sleep, and don't participate in any fast-arm sports such as tennis or golf.

10. Eat a well-balanced muscle-building diet that includes plenty of protein from meat, fish, eggs, cheese, and milk. Be sure to eat only the best fresh fruits and vegetables for the natural carbohydrate energy you need for heavy training.

11. Stay away from junk foods and highly processed foods, which are practically useless for building muscle size.

12. Don't do more than two arm workouts a week on this arduous program. Three will be too much, and not only will you burn out quickly, but you may even get smaller.

"If you are ready for it," said Sergio, "this program can take your arms from 17 or so inches at the start and blast them into 20-inchers and beyond—and maybe, someday, all the way to the Mr. Universe and Mr. Olympia titles!"

Chapter 19

DINOSAUR TRAINING
THE SECRETS TO BUILDING JURASSIC SIZE AND STRENGTH

BY BROOKS D. KUBIK

For nearly 30 years, Bradley J. Steiner has been saying in *Ironman* magazine that the old-time methods of building muscle and strength have much to offer modern trainees. I agree with that 100 percent. That's one reason I wrote a book called *Dinosaur Training: Lost Secrets of Strength and Development*. Sales have been extremely good, so, apparently, lots of other people are at least curious about how the old-timers' training might benefit modern lifters.

Others, however, aren't convinced that the old-timers actually knew very much about training. After all, today's bodybuilders are so much bigger and more cut than their counterparts of yesteryear. Why would aspiring trainees in the late 1990s want to check out their training methods?

Scan the following paragraphs and ask yourself if you know anyone who can match the feats described.

Hermann Goerner

On October 8, 1928, in Leipzig, Germany, at a bodyweight of 220 pounds, Goerner did a one-arm deadlift with 727.5 pounds. At a relatively modest size compared with today's superheavyweights, Goerner could do a one-arm barbell clean with 297.62 pounds, a strict barbell curl with 220.46, a right-hand snatch with 264.55, a right-hand swing with two kettle bells weighing a total of 220.46 pounds, a continental-style clean of 440.92 pounds, a two-hand clean and jerk of 390.22 pounds, and a two-arm snatch with his arms crossed with 231. I'd like to see any modern lifter—at any bodyweight—on or off steroids duplicate those feats.

Arthur Saxon

At a body weight of around 210 pounds, Arthur Saxon could juggle 119-pound kettle bells, bent-press 370, lift 448 in the "two hands anyhow," and bent-press a 300-pound barbell, stand erect with the weight, then toss it from one hand to the other. On one occasion, he bent-pressed 297.6 pounds using only his little finger (the weight was suspended from a strong leather loop around the finger). Saxon could

Hermann Goerner.

Otto Arco

Arco weighed between 135 and 138 pounds, but he could continental clean and jerk 278.5—more than double his bodyweight— and jerk 305 when the weight was handed to him at his shoulders. His physique was so impressive that he posed for the world-famous sculptor Auguste Rodin. In 1913, in Paris, he won the title of World's Most Perfectly Developed Man. In his specialty, Herculean hand-balancing, Arco was unrivaled. He could hold his partner overhead in a hand-to-hand balance, kneel down, lie on his back, roll over, and then work his way back to his feet—holding the hand-to-hand balance through the entire maneuver. None of the guys from the Eastern European camp—or any other modern lifters—can top that one.

Paul Anderson.

snatch with one hand a rough wooden plank that was 10 inches wide, 3 inches thick, and 15 feet long and weighed 90 pounds. He could lift overhead a 300-pound bag of flour, a feat he dared all challengers to beat throughout his career as a circus and music-hall strongman. To no surprise, no one ever did. How many modern guys fresh off their latest periodization program can duplicate those performances?

Early-1900s strongmen, such as Al Treloar, were capable of incredible feats, such as back lifting huge poundages of people and machinery. (circa 1920)

Maxick

Maxick was born on June 28, 1882, stood 5′ 3¼″, and weighed 145 to 147 pounds in his prime. At that bodyweight, he performed the following lifts: right-hand snatch, 165 pounds; right-hand swing, 150; right-hand jerk—after shouldering the barbell with two hands—240; two-hand military press, 230; two-hand clean and jerk with barbell, 272; two-hand continental clean and jerk, 340. He pressed a 185-pound man (Tromp Von Diggelen) overhead 16 times with one arm while holding in his other hand a glass of beer filled to the brim, from which he spilled not a drop. On another occasion, he held the apparently fearless Von Diggelen overhead with one hand and ran up and down two flights of stairs. By way of comparison, a right-hand jerk of 240 pounds at a bodyweight of less than 150 is equivalent to a modern-day Mr. Everything at a bodyweight of maybe 215 doing a one-arm jerk with 344 pounds.

Is it possible that the feats performed by Saxon, Arco, Goerner, and Maxick could aid you in your quest for greater muscular size and strength? If your answer to that question is in the affirmative—and I submit that there's no other reasonable answer—keep reading.

Maxick (left) and two of his students show amazing presteroid, presupplement development. (circa 1910)

DINOSAUR EXERCISES

Have you noticed how many tried-and-true free-weight exercises are falling into oblivion? Many of the best movements ever developed are not only no longer practiced but also are fast becoming unknown. These include the bent press, of course, and virtually all the rest of the old-time one-arm lifts: the one-arm clean, one-arm press, one-arm snatch, one-arm swing, and one-arm deadlift. Kettle-bell training is almost a lost art.

It's not just the obscure old-style exercises that are in danger of becoming extinct, however. Take the deadlift, for example. How many men do deadlifts anymore? Not counting powerlifters, the answer is: darned few. Nowadays you can go to almost any commercial gym and train deadlifts, and guys will come up and ask what you're doing. They'll think it's some kind of cheating bent-over row, and some will even tell you that seated cable rows work better and are a much safer exercise for your lats.

Other terrific exercises that are all but forgotten include the snatch, the clean and jerk, the power clean, the high pull, and the halting deadlift. When was the last time you saw a guy do halting deadlifts?

Even the stiff-legged deadlift is in danger. That was one of the great exercises covered in the old Milo barbell courses—just check out Bill Hinbern's reprints of the course if you don't believe me. It's one of the movements that made John Grimek immortal (he could handle more than 400 pounds for reps).

Maurice Jones of Canada was another old-time iron monster who handled huge poundages on stiff-legged deadlifts and got as big and strong as a horse. Dr. Ken Leistner used to rave about them. So did John McCallum, among others. Who today besides Bradley Steiner champions this exercise? Hardly anyone? If the deadlift is included in a routine, it's supposed to be performed with baby weights as part of a 30-to-40-set "back blitz" or part of a superset with leg curls to pump those little thigh biceps.

How about the military press? When did you last see someone at a commercial gym or college weight room do overhead presses with a barbell? Nowadays any overhead presses are performed with dumbbells, usually while seated, or else done seated on a machine. There was a time—and it wasn't too long ago—when the question, What can you press? referred to your military press. Today the only thing anyone asks about is the bench press. Most guys have no idea how heavy they can go on the military press. They have no idea of the terrific benefits to be gained from heavy standing presses.

No one ever does standing straight-bar curls, either. People think they're too basic, so they replace them with cable curls, dumbbell concentration curls, seated dumbbell curls, or machine curls. If they do standing curls, they always use an EZ-curl bar.

The good morning. The wrestler's bridge. Neck work with a head strap. Sit-ups. Leg raises. Side bends with a heavy dumbbell. All practically on the point of extinction.

That goes for the parallel squat, too. Aside from the lifters, you can go to many gyms and never see anyone do real squats. If people do get under a squat bar, they're darned careful to keep the movement to four inches—often with 150 on their shoulders. Can you imagine? The single most productive exercise in existence, and the percentage of weight trainers who perform it is ridiculously low.

As a Dinosaur trainer, you owe it to the greats of yesterday—the pioneers of the iron game—to keep the grand old exercises alive. Continue the tradition—and you'll

find yourself reaping benefits of historic proportions.

While I don't have room to detail specialization programs for building all your bodyparts to monster proportions, the following arm routine will give you an idea of how Dinosaur Training works.

DINOSAUR TRAINING UNLEASHED: FORMULA FOR JURASSIC ARMS

Do you want enormous arms that pulsate with strength and power—arms that not only look strong but are strong? Get ready to work harder than you've ever worked in your life.

Follow this program religiously—exactly as written—for the next 12 weeks, and your arms will swell with increased power and size. You should also make good gains in overall development, total-body strength, and muscular bodyweight.

Train three days per week using a Monday-Wednesday-Friday or Tuesday-Thursday-Saturday schedule. I know that doesn't sound like much, but, believe me, if you work as hard as this program requires, you won't want to hit the iron any more frequently.

Workout 1

Start with any kind of general aerobic warm-up—skip rope, jog in place, do a couple of quick sets of light cleans or snatches, or use a stationary bicycle or stair machine for 5 to 10 minutes. Don't kill yourself on the warm-up—just do enough to get your heart and lungs working, your blood circulating, and a bit of sweat going.

Start the workout with six sets of five reps on the parallel squat. Do three progressively heavier warm-up sets, then do three work sets with your top poundage. For example, let's say you can do five reps with 300 pounds. You might do 150 for five, 200 for five, and 250 for five on your warm-up sets and then shoot for three sets of five with 300 pounds. If you can't get five reps on each of your three work sets, that's OK. As long as you get a total of at least 12 reps, stay with that poundage and build up over time. Once you can get three sets of five with a certain weight, add 5 or 10 pounds to the bar the next time you squat.

After the squats, do bench presses. Use the 6 × 5 system on them, as well.

Lat pulldowns or chins—preferably with extra weight tied around your waist—are next. Use the grip that lets you handle the most weight. For me, a parallel grip is best, but some people do better with other variations. Do the pulldowns to your chest, as the behind-the-neck version can cause shoulder problems. If you're chinning, pull to the chest as well.

Now it's time for some arm training, Dinosaur-style. You begin with a classic triceps bulker, close-grip bench presses, but you do them with a special technique. For starters, use a 3-inch-diameter bar instead of a standard 1-inch or 1¹/₁₆-inch bar. A thick-handled bar is enormously more difficult to lift than a

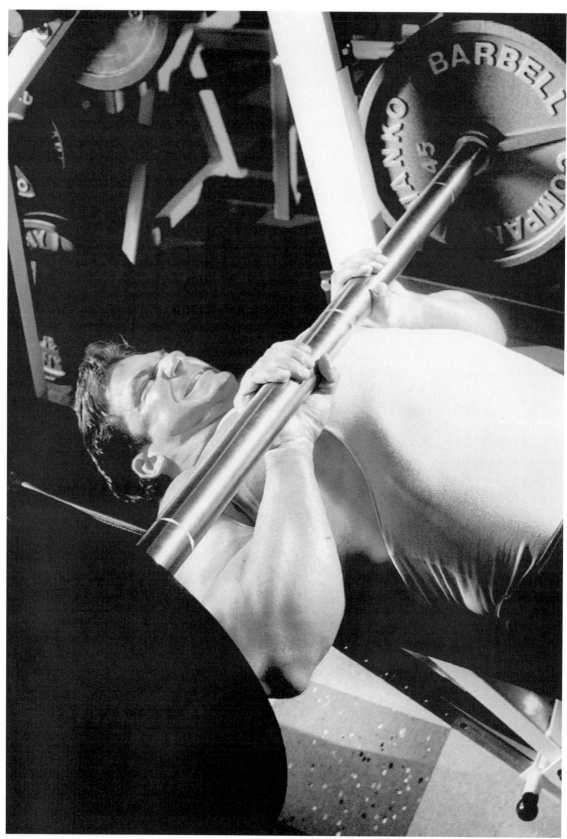

Close-grip bench presses.

regular-size bar. The secret of successful training is hard work. No matter how hard you can train with a regular bar, you can train harder if you use a thick-handled one. You'll trigger stronger and more numerous nerve impulses and contract more muscle fibers, which adds up to big gains in strength and development.

Where do you get such a bar? You can buy one from Ironmind Enterprises: (916) 265-6725. Alternatively, you can hire a welder to make one for you out of strong steel pipe.

Use a power rack for your close-grip benches. Set the pins so that the bar brushes against your chest in the bottom position, and start each rep at the bottom. That makes it a far more difficult movement than the traditional style of bench pressing in which you begin with your arms locked and lower the bar to your chest.

The power rack is for safety. A thick-handled barbell is as hard to handle as a tele-phone pole. It's very easy for it to slip out of your hands. Consequently, you'd be insane to lift one over your head unless you were using a power rack. You don't want to take any chance of having the bar drop on your face.

Use the same 6 × 5 system on the close grips that you used on the other exercises. Take a shoulder-width grip. Doing the movement with your hands any closer than that will limit your training poundages tremendously. In addition, it's a great way to injure a wrist or elbow.

After the close grips, you do some Dinosaur-style arm curls. These call for a heavy sandbag. That's right—a sandbag. They're easy to make. Buy an old Army surplus duffel bag and two or three 50-pound sandbags, and you're in business. The total cost for a 150-pound sandbag is around $25, so don't wimp out and try to get by with concentration curls or similar nonsense just

Paul DeMayo starting a squat.

Squats, finish.

Barbell curls.

because you want to save a couple of bucks. In a pinch, you can substitute the thick-handled barbell when the program calls for the sandbag, but if you're serious about training—and I assume you are or you wouldn't be reading this—the cost of a heavy sandbag or a thick-handled barbell is not going to be a big deal.

Sandbag curls are a brutal exercise for the entire arm. They work you from shoulder to fingertips. The leverage of a heavy sandbag is much different from that of a barbell. The last couple of inches of a sandbag curl are extremely difficult because the bulk of the bag isn't close to your body. Instead of encountering a sticking point at the middle of the movement and having the exercise get easier at the end, which is what happens with a barbell, you hit a hard sticking point when your forearms are parallel to the floor, and it gets worse with every inch you go.

Of course, your grip and forearms get a tremendous workout because of the difficulty of grabbing the bag and digging in for the entire set. You won't need to do anything extra for your forearms and grip if you work hard on sandbag curls.

Use the same sets-and-reps scheme on the sandbag curls that you used on the other exercises—three progressively heavier warm-up sets followed by three work sets with your top weight, all for five reps per set.

Workout 2

Begin with a light aerobic warm-up for 5 to 10 minutes—exactly the same as you did at Workout 1. The first exercise is the close-grip bench presses described in the previous section—performed in a power rack with the thick-handled barbell, starting from your chest and pushing up to arms' length. The big change this time around is that you do singles on the movement. That's right—only one rep per set. Start light, and work up to a weight that's around 90 to 95 percent of your top weight. Do five or six sets, starting with progressively heavier warm-ups and working up to your final set, the heaviest effort of the day.

Dinosaurs love single-rep training. Heavy singles enable you to work your muscles, ten-

Hammer curls.

dons, and ligaments with the heaviest possible weight—and no matter what you may have heard to the contrary, it takes heavy weights to build big muscles. Forget about the "pumping" and "feeling" stuff. You'll be surprised at how much weight you can use on your exercises if you pay your dues and sweat blood for a couple of years. I'm up to 400 pounds on the close-grip bench press with a three-inch-thick bar, and I'm probably old enough to be your father, if not your grandfather.

The next exercise is single-rep barbell curls performed with a thick-handled barbell. Do four to five progressively heavier singles, and work up to your top weight for the day—close to 90 to 95 percent of your top weight on the curl.

You may find that a three-inch bar is too thick for heavy curls. (If you have small hands, that will definitely be the case.) The solution is to use a two-inch bar, which means you may have to buy or make two thick-handled bars, one for benches and one for curls. Remember, though, that you're after some serious results, and your results can be only as good as your equipment. Train with ordinary equipment, and you'll get ordinary results.

Follow the curls with heavy overhead presses performed with your sandbag or with a barbell. Use the same weight on each set, and do five sets of as many reps as possible. Try to pick a weight that lets you get 8 to 10 reps on the first set, and work like heck to get at least 5 reps on each ensuing set. That may not sound like much, but if you take the first set to total muscular failure, the weight will feel like a ton on each of the following sets, especially if you use a sandbag. The overhead press performed with a heavy sandbag is a real man-maker and will give your delts and triceps a hammering that's so hard, you can't even imagine it.

After the overhead presses, do sandbag curls—or regular-bar curls—for five sets of as

Standing military presses.

Incline dumbbell presses.

many reps as possible. Use a weight that lets you get 8 to 10 reps on the first set, just as you did with the presses, and try to get at least 5 reps on each of the following sets. That will be really tough to do as you get tired, and believe me, this baby will make you very tired very quickly.

Following every set you do in this program, be sure you're well rested before you begin your next set. Your goal is not to race the clock. You're training for strength, so take it slowly. Two or three minutes between sets is about right for most exercises. On extremely demanding ones—squats, for example—you may need a five-minute rest between work sets.

Finish the session by hanging from a chinning bar for as long as possible. It's a great exercise for the hands, fingers, and forearms. As you get stronger, tie extra weight around your waist—or better yet, switch to a thicker chinning bar. Hanging from a two-inch bar is sheer torture, but it will build a world-class grip in short order.

Stiff-legged deadlifts.

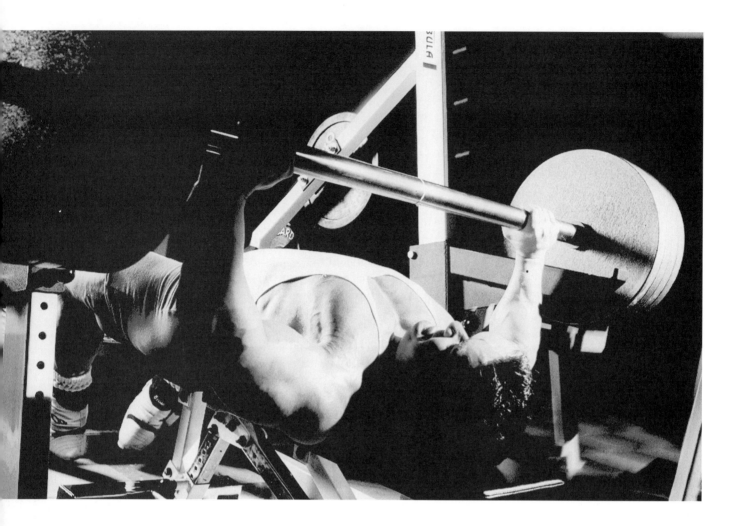

Workout 3

Once again, you begin with a short aerobic warm-up. The first movement is six sets of five reps on one of the following exercises: deadlifts, stiff-legged deadlifts, partial deadlifts from the knees, dumbbell deadlifts, power cleans, or power pulls. There are many good exercises for the back, and most people have a definite preference for one or another, due largely to inherited structural characteristics. Find a heavy back exercise that works well for you, and stick to it.

If there's a trap bar available, use it for your deadlifts. The trap bar makes deadlifts much more productive, more efficient, and safer for almost everyone.

Next, do one of the following: incline dumbbell presses, regular-grip bench presses with the three-inch bar, or dips. If you choose

the thick-bar benches, do them in the power rack, starting from your chest, with the pins set to catch the bar if it slips. Continue with the 6 × 5 system that you used throughout the week.

Follow the presses with hammer curls using two heavy dumbbells. Again, do six sets of five reps. For best results, use thick-handled dumbbells. They're easy to make: simply wrap tape around the handles of ordinary dumbbells, and then slide a small length of two-inch steel pipe over the tape. You can also buy thick-handled dumbbells from Ironmind Enterprises: (916) 265-6725.

After the hammer curls, do bench press lockouts in the power rack, using the three-inch bar. Set the pins so that you lift the bar about four to five inches on each rep. Do six sets of five, working slowly and carefully. Do not bounce the bar off of the pins so you can get more reps or handle more weight, as it will move you out of the groove, diminish your results, and quite possibly lead to an injury. Bouncing the bar off of the pins is a form of cheating. It makes the exercise easier, which is exactly what you don't want.

Finish the workout with the farmer's walk: grab a pair of heavy dumbbells, hold them at your sides with straight arms, and walk as far as possible. If you can do it outside, go for distance. If you do it indoors, walk back and forth, and go for time. Do one or two sets of the farmer's walk, and your forearms will ache and swell beyond belief.

As an alternative, grab a heavy sandbag, hold it in a bear hug, and walk as far as possible. Do that for two to three sets, and you'll discover a new meaning to the phrase *hard work*. You'll also get a great arm, shoulder, forearm, and grip workout.

It's a simple program, but don't let that fool you. Work hard on it, and you'll be tired and sore. You'll also grow like corn in Iowa.

Use your head, and break in the Dinosaur routine slowly and steadily. Take a couple of weeks to work up to weights that make you sweat, then train hard and heavy for 10 to 12 weeks. Get plenty of rest, and eat lots of good food—especially protein and complex carbs. While you're on the program, try to eat at least one gram of protein for every two pounds of bodyweight. If you're under the age of 25, add another 50 to 75 grams of protein per day.

Dinosaur Training is all about using heavy poundages and working hard. In general, you want to make your training progressive; that is, add weight to the bar—or the sandbag—whenever possible. Always maintain good form, but don't be afraid to add weight to the bar. Nobody ever got big and strong by using bunny weights.

The foregoing no-nonsense formula for building muscular, power-packed arms should give you an idea of the intensity you can achieve when you train like the old iron masters.

Power cleans.

Regular deadlifts.

DINOSAUR ARM PROGRAM

Unless otherwise indicated, do three progressively heavier warm-up sets, followed by three work sets with your top weight. Train on Monday, Wednesday, and Friday.

Day 1

Aerobic warm-up	× 5–10 minutes
Parallel squats	6 × 5
Bench presses	6 × 5
Lat pulldowns or weighted chins	6 × 5
Bottom-position close-grip bench presses*	6 × 5
Sandbag or thick-bar curls	6 × 5

Day 2

Aerobic warm-up	× 5–10 minutes
Bottom-position close-grip bench presses*	5–6 × 1
Thick-bar curls	5–6 × 1
Sandbag or barbell overhead presses	5 × failure
Sandbag or thick-bar curls	5 × failure
Hang from chinning bar	1 × failure

Day 3

Aerobic warm-up	× 5–10 minutes
Deadlifts, stiff-legged deadlifts, partial deadlifts from knees, dumbbell deadlifts, power cleans, or power pulls	6 × 5
Incline dumbbell presses, flat-bench thick-bar presses,* flat-bench dumbbell presses, or dips	6 × 5
Hammer curls**	6 × 5
Bench press lockouts*	6 × 5
Farmer's walk	1–2 × failure
or sandbag walk	2–3 × failure

*Performed with a thick bar in a power rack.

**Preferably using thick-handled dumbbells.

Weighted chins.

ONE-ARM DEADLIFT

A question from a Dinosaur trainee highlights one of the great exercises of all time, now almost extinct.

> I'm a competitive powerlifter, and while my bench numbers are OK, my squat and deadlift poundages are stagnating. I've tried several different training systems on each lift and lots of assistance exercises, but nothing seems to work. I feel I need more power in the middle of my body to handle my top weights, but I just can't seem to build it where I want it. I'm also having trouble holding on to the bar when I train deadlifts or when I'm in a meet. Do you have any advice?

The one-arm deadlift could very well be the ticket to your power-lifting success. It offers three important benefits for power-lifters: it builds a viselike grip, it hits the lats as no other exercise can, and it builds tremendous strength in the stabilizing muscle. In terms of grip strength, it's perhaps the single best movement for developing crushing power in the hands and fingers, which means you'll never miss a deadlift because your grip gives out.

Once you get the hang of the one-arm deadlift, you'll be able to handle well in excess of 50 percent of your top weight on the two-hand deadlift, and 70 percent is definitely within reach if you train hard on the one-hand movement. Think of what that means as far as overloading your grip. If you deadlift 600 pounds on the conventional movement, your hands divide the poundage equally: each hand has to hold 300 pounds. If you train one-arm deadlifts until you can pull 70 percent of your 600-pound maximum, that's 420 pounds. Each hand is lifting 120 pounds more than it lifts when you do the two-hand version.

Now consider the lat-bombing benefit. What do you handle for pulldowns? Two hundred pounds? Two fifty? Even if you can handle 300 pounds, that's only 150 pounds on each side, compared with what you can do on the one-arm deadlift.

The same principle applies to one-arm dumbbell rows. Think how much more of a contribution your lats will make to your two-arm deadlifts if they can help pull and stabilize 400 or more pounds on the one-arm deadlift.

One-arm deadlifts.

As for the tremendous strength that the exercise builds in the stabilizers that cross and interconnect the upper thighs, lower back, hips, sides, and abdominals, you develop a corset of steel that girdles your entire waist. You get a muscular effect that mimics the tight, solid support of a squat suit and lifting belt.

That's particularly true if you do your one-arm deadlifts suitcase-style—that is, while standing to the side of the bar. Most lifters straddle the bar, and some lift with the bar in front of them—as they would for a regular deadlift. The suitcase-style one-arm deadlift has particular benefits for powerlifters because it hits the obliques and the lower-back-and-hip tie-ins harder than any other exercise, including side bends with heavy weights. Think of how much more secure you'd be under a heavy squat bar if the muscles that support your sides, hips, and lower back were as hard as granite and strong enough to handle a 300-pound one-arm suitcase-style deadlift.

When I perform this exercise, I usually begin with the straddle style, and I use a cambered bar, as it's much easier to balance than a straight bar. The Buffalo Bar sold by Ironmind Enterprises and the McDonald bench press bar both work well for this exercise. If you use a kettle-bell handle and a five- or six-foot bar, you'll find that the balance on the lift is a breeze. With that type of equipment, you should make it into the 400-pound club (if you weigh more than 165 pounds) or the double-weight club (if you're lighter than 165).

Use a shoulder-width stance, or go slightly wider. Lock your lower back, torso muscles, and lats, then reach down, flex the triceps on the lifting arm to keep it straight, hold your back flat, and grab the bar exactly in the center. If you miss the center by even a half inch, you'll probably miss the lift.

Brace the nonlifting hand on your knee. This is critical. When you start the pull, drive your heels through the floor just as you would on a normal deadlift, then pull with the lifting hand and push down hard with the hand that's braced on your knee. Nothing will happen at first. Then slowly and majestically, the bar will leave the floor.

Pull it to just above your knees, pause, then lower it carefully. Never lift the bar above that point because your thighs will straighten out, and there will be nothing to support the nonlifting hand. The nonlifting hand, which provides plenty of support for the initial pull, will suddenly drop out of the picture, leaving the rest of your body to cope with a sudden shift in the load and leaving your lower back and your sides vulnerable to injury.

Here's another key point: Always do singles on the one-arm deadlift. You cannot maintain the proper balance and groove if you do multiple reps. That goes for warm-up sets, too.

To perform the exercise suitcase-style, stand with your feet at shoulder width or a little farther apart; lock your lower back and torso muscles and your lats; flex the triceps on the lifting arm to hold it in place; brace the nonlifting hand on your knee, grab the bar, and pull. In this case, you want to pull it to where your body is fully erect. Due to the difference in leverage, I find that I can safely stand fully erect on this version. Be aware, however, that the lift won't feel easy. There are no sweet spots. It starts hard and ends hard. Standing erect with 200 or more pounds hanging at arm's length from one hand is sheer torture for the torso and trunk muscles.

If you want to give one-arm deadlifts a try, start out light, learn the movement, build up slowly, and train with your head rather than your emotions. Once you get the feel of it, you can start to add weight—and get the full benefit of this great exercise.

THICK-BAR POWER HOLDS

Grip training is one of the forgotten secrets of strength and development. Most modern lifters are almost totally clueless about this area. They do either wrist curls and reverse wrist curls or wrist curls and reverse curls. Those are fine exercises, but they don't build the kind of crushing grip power that marks a human powerhouse. For a Dinosaur grip, you need to do lots of specialized grip work on exercises that most people have never heard of.

Thick-bar power holds.

The old-timers like the men described earlier were grip monsters, and you can be sure they didn't get that way by pumping out high-rep sets of wrist curls or reverse curls with poundages your aunt Matilda would laugh at. They trained heavy. They used low reps. They hit their hands, fingers, forearms, and wrists from many different angles. You may not develop the strength to deadlift 727.5 pounds with one hand, as Hermann Goerner did, but you can increase your gripping power tremendously.

Start by doing power holds. You need a barbell with a handle that's at least two inches thick. For many men, two and a half inches will be even better—although three would be too much for these exercises.

Once you have your bar, use the power rack to set it just above your knees. Position it as though you were going to do a top-position deadlift in the rack. If you don't have a power rack, use concrete blocks or a heavy-duty wooden platform under the barbell plates to raise the bar to the required height. Or you can just do the movement off the floor—but pad the floor if you do! If you perform the movement correctly, you're going to drop the bar at the end of each set.

After the bar is in position, load it to 135 pounds or so. If you have a real good grip, go heavier—perhaps up to 200.

Get into position as though you were going to deadlift the bar, and take an overhand grip. Do not use the reverse grip that you use when you deadlift in competition—that would defeat the purpose of the exercise. To train your grip, you want to make it as hard as possible to hold on to the bar.

Of course, you won't use straps on this exercise. That, too, would defeat the purpose.

Hold the bar with your hands slightly wider than your thighs. You don't want to be able to jam your thumbs back against your thighs for assistance. You want your grip to be taxed to its utmost.

Lift the bar off the pins, and hold it for as long as possible. Hold it until your hands, fingers, and forearms are screaming in agony, and then hold it some more. Time yourself. Compete with your training partners. Give it

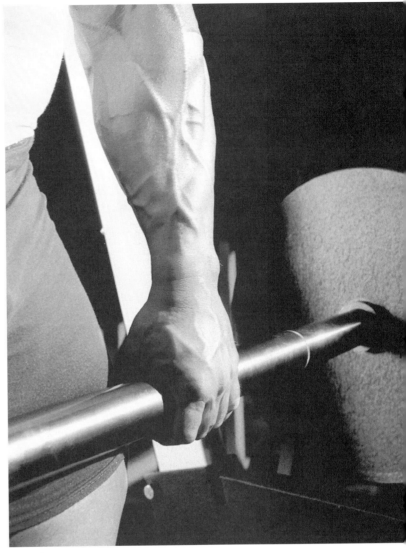

Thick bar.

everything you have. Hold the bar until it literally drops out of your exhausted fingers and crashes to the pins.

Rest a couple of minutes, and then repeat the exercise. Once again, go for broke.

I call these power holds. They're simple but amazingly effective and will lay the foundation for the development of truly ferocious gripping power. Start doing several sets of power holds, finishing with a burnout set or two with the SuperGripper, two or three times a week for a couple of months. Your hands may not love you for it, but they'll certainly respond by growing real strong real quick.

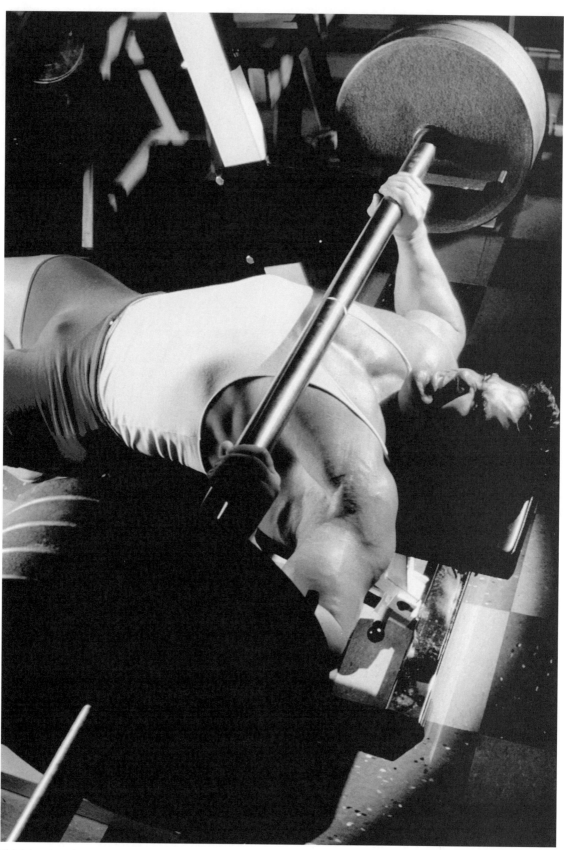

Thick-bar bench presses.

Thick-bar barbell curls.

BOTTOM-POSITION BENCH PRESSES

The arm routine I described earlier features bottom-position bench presses, which are performed in a power rack, or off an adjustable squat rack, with the catcher pins positioned so that you can place the bar where it will brush your chest in the bottom position, and you begin the movement from the bottom—pushing up to arm's length to complete it.

That's the only way I've trained the bench press for years, and I doubt if I will ever go back to the regular style. The bottom-position bench is far more difficult, far more productive, and far safer.

I discovered this exercise more or less by accident. I'd read about bottom-position rack work ever since I was a kid—Tony Ditillo used to give it good reviews—but I never had enough brains to give it a try.

When I was around 31 or 32, I was training at a commercial gym in Louisville, and I

tried a 430-pound touch-and-go bench press. There was one experienced spotter behind the bench, so I felt safe. The bar went down and started up like a flash. Then it started to sputter and stumble, and it ground to an awkward almost halt nearly halfway up. I kept pushing and probably would have made it, but suddenly a "helpful" gym member ran over and grabbed the right side of the bar.

He later explained that I looked as if I was struggling, and he wanted to make sure I didn't hurt myself.

Hurt myself? The idiot almost tore my shoulder out of the socket. You can imagine what it's like to be benching more than 400 pounds and have someone pull up as hard as possible on one side of the bar.

I didn't kill him, but I should have. The guy I was really mad at was the spotter, who never said a word to call the guy off when he ran up to the bar. "I didn't know what to say," he told me later.

"What about, 'Don't touch the bar'?" I suggested.

The bottom line was, I decided that the gym was too crazy a place for me to continue to bench outside of the rack there. I began to do all of my benching in the rack, starting from the bottom and pushing up and back to a complete lockout. That way, I never had to worry about spotters, safety, or helpful lunatics.

Because I found it awkward to do reps in the rack, I started to do heavy singles. Thus, as the result of training in a gym populated by negligent spotters and overly helpful morons,

I stumbled onto two basic principles of Dinosaur Training: single-rep work and bottom-position rack work.

The combination proved its merit almost immediately. It worked so well that I decided to try it on the squat. That worked so well, I put more than 100 pounds on my all-time-best lift in about eight or nine months. After that, I was sold. Give bottom-position bench presses and squats a try, and see how they work for you.

Bench presses.

Chapter 20

6× NUTRITION FOR XL RESULTS

BY MICHAEL GÜNDILL

Newcomers to the weight-lifting community are usually amazed at the bodybuilding lifestyle. One of the things that surprises them the most is how often bodybuilders eat. The six-meals-per-day regimen isn't a maximum; it's a minimum, and many bodybuilders get up to eat during the night. The question is, Do bodybuilders really have to eat that often? Is there any scientific basis to the six-meals-a-day concept?

ACCELERATING THE ANABOLIC DRIVE

The ultimate goal for a bodybuilder is to pack on lean mass. The very first bodybuilders figured out that to bulk up, they had to eat as much as possible, and that meant they had to eat more frequently. There was simply no way they could ingest enough food with only the three traditional meals.

They got big, but they also got fat. Modern bodybuilders reasoned that if they kept the frequency but dropped the excessive calories, they could remain leaner while growing larger. This concept is well illustrated in a Russian study by V. N. Litvinova, who discovered that when he spread the food intake of rats over five meals rather than three, their rate of muscle protein synthesis increased.[1] That's exactly what bodybuilders want.

Look at it from this perspective: If you're not eating, you're fasting, and no one ever got bigger and stronger by fasting. Assuming that it takes 3 hours to digest a meal, if you eat only three times a day, you're eating for 9 hours and fasting for 15. So, you spend most of the day fasting—and in a catabolic state. If you eat six times a day, however, you eat for 12 to 18 hours, depending on the kinds of protein and carbs you take in. Fasting represents only 6 to 12 hours, which is still too much, but it's far less than 15 hours.

HOW MEALS CAN CONTROL PROTEIN SYNTHESIS

Remember that muscle mass is subject to a constant protein turnover. Old proteins are degraded (catabolism) while new ones are formed (anabolism). Meals stimulate muscle protein synthesis; fasting reduces it. By the same token, meals reduce catabolism; fasting enhances it. As a result, meals make your muscles bigger, and fasting makes them smaller. Equate muscle with meals, and you'll be on the right bodybuilding track.

You may wonder how eating or not eating can affect the protein turnover so dramatically. The intracellular machinery responsible for muscle protein synthesis is cumbersome, but it can be stopped or activated quickly at the initiation level. Inside each muscle cell are many little "machines" that make new proteins. If the machines work rapidly enough, new proteins, which are responsible for muscle contractions, will accumulate, and your muscles will get bigger and stronger. Each anabolic machine has two switches: one to turn it on and one to turn it off. The on button initiates the machine's action, and scientists call those initiators eIF4E, for eukaryotic initiation factor 4E. The more free eIF4E there is inside your muscle cells, the stronger the anabolic drive will be.

The off button, which stops the initiation, is called 4E-BP1. The BP, or binding protein, is just like IGF-BP1, a protein that binds to the hormone IGF. When binding proteins bind to a molecule, they usually trap and inactivate it. Whenever 4E-BP1 binds to eIF4E, it forms a complex called eIF4E.4E-BP1. As a result, the free eIF4E is now trapped and cannot switch on the muscle-building machines. Therefore, eIF4E represents the bottleneck of muscle protein synthesis—where anabolism is either switched on or switched off in the short term.

As you eat protein, the amino acids it contains free your eIF4E from the 4E-BP1. That's how most of the anabolic influences of dietary proteins work.[2] New research suggests that amino acids may also directly reduce the production of another binding protein, IGF1-BP1, which prevents IGF-1 from producing its muscle-building effects.[3] Therefore, amino acids also have a positive effect on your anabolic hormone levels and the growth reactions that they produce.

It's easy to understand that the more your muscles are exposed to amino acids, the more free eIF4E will initiate anabolism. Nevertheless, you have to reach a certain amino acid threshold to free enough eIF4E to increase anabolism significantly. Whey protein, which is absorbed

HOW MEALS CAN CONTROL CATABOLISM

Whenever the blood level of amino acids rises but not to the anabolic threshold, it stops catabolism and has almost no effect on anabolism. Proteins like casein, which don't come close to reaching the anabolic threshold, are good at providing long-lasting muscle protection because of their slow, gradual absorption. Whenever a muscle doesn't get its basic supply of exogenous amino acids from the diet, it will cannibalize itself to provide new muscle-building blocks. Casein offers a long-lasting guarantee against that cannibalization, thanks to its natural time-release action. Insulin is also responsible in part for the meal-induced reduction in catabolism. Insulin is usually an anticatabolic hormone, except right after training. Fasting produces a lack of insulin, which rapidly triggers catabolism.

BOOSTING YOUR TOTAL PROTEIN INTAKE

The point of the 6× nutrition program is not only to supply nutrients more uniformly but also to boost your total protein intake. Everyone knows that the digestive tract's ability to absorb proteins is limited, and the common belief is that you can digest no more than 30 grams of protein in a three-hour period. Who in his or her right mind, however, believes that champions like Nasser El Sonbaty can handle only 10 grams of protein per hour? Measure 10 grams of whey, and judge for yourself.

Today's protein powders make it possible for your body to absorb more protein. That's especially true with high-quality whey or casein products. They're predigested, so all you have to do is open your mouth and swallow, and amino acids enter your bloodstream almost immediately. Research has shown that significant amounts of whey or casein are in your blood within 20 minutes of ingestion. It doesn't take hours to absorb them. Two hours after administration, however, whey is long gone, while casein is still there, producing anticatabolic actions.

rapidly, is the easiest and most efficient means of reaching that anabolic threshold. It's superior for increasing protein synthesis because it provides a pharmacological level of amino acids that's called hyperaminoacidemia.

The hormone insulin also has the ability to free the eIF4E to some extent. Its effects are weaker than those of amino acids, but it can work wonders in combination with amino acids.

When you fast, your blood's amino acid level is reduced. Increasingly more eIF4E becomes locked by the 4E-BP1, and your anabolic drive slows. So, to free the eIF4E, you eat protein; to trap it, you fast.

The blood protein level acts as an accelerator or a brake for anabolism: low protein equals low anabolism, and high protein equals high anabolism. Naturally, you want to speed up anabolism as often as possible, so you have to ingest protein frequently. That's the rationale behind the 6× nutrition plan. You get to accelerate anabolism during most of the day instead of braking often, as you do on a traditional three-meals-a-day plan.

A high speed of absorption, as you get with whey protein, requires that you eat very frequently. Today's high-tech proteins are wasted if you eat only three times a day because they enter and leave your system so quickly. Even the more recent recommendation of eating every three waking hours can be inefficient if you use only fast-absorbing whey protein. The slower and harder-to-digest milk-and-egg mixture is better suited to the every-three-hours scenario. While the introduction of whey allowed bodybuilders to reach a new, higher level of protein absorption, it also meant that six meals a day weren't enough for experienced bodybuilders using mostly whey protein. In that case, 10 meals would be better for maintaining an anabolic state.

The solution is to introduce high-quality, slower-absorbing casein. A whey-and-casein combination allows you to stay within the less constraining confines of the six-meals-a-day regimen.

Compared with three normal meals, which bring in at most 150 grams of protein a day, six meals can help you take in more than 250 grams. Advanced drug-using bodybuilders can build up to 10 meals a day to reach the 400-gram mark, but that's excessive for natural bodybuilders. Steroids increase the need for protein because they accelerate muscle-protein turnover. What's more, many steroid users have to reduce their carb intake, or they blow up because of the excessive water retention that the drugs can induce. That means they must increase protein to recoup the calorie deficit created by lower-carb diets.

WHY LOSE DURING THE NIGHT WHAT WAS SO PAINFULLY GAINED DURING THE DAY?

A common misconception among weight lifters is that your body builds muscle mass while you sleep. During your nocturnal fast, your muscles become net exporters of amino acids, which means you're in a catabolic phase. More eIF4E.4E-BP1 complexes are formed, slowing the anabolic drive. So, while a minimal anabolic response repairs some of the muscle damage inflicted by training, the overall balance is usually negative due to nocturnal catabolism. You can recover faster and grow more if you tame it.

you tend to wake up in the middle of the night anyway—say, to go to the bathroom—have another whey-and-casein drink. In either case, remember that the first thing you want to do in the morning is free your eIF4E with a huge whey-protein drink. That will jump-start your anabolism and partly make up for the night-time slowdown.

WATCH YOUR CALORIES

Bodybuilders have to eat more frequently than other people, but that doesn't mean you have to eat more calories. You just have to spread your calorie intake more uniformly throughout the day. Eating frequently allows you to increase your protein dramatically, but you should compensate for those extra protein calories by reducing carb or fat calories. Studies have shown that a better allocation of your daily food intake can allow you to eat slightly more without gaining fat.[4] (That was

The first way of taming nocturnal catabolism is to have a casein or casein-and-whey shake right before bed. The timed release of amino acids will protect your muscles. Of course, eating carbs along with the casein would accentuate the anticatabolic effect, but the problem is that it's fattening to eat carbs at night. It's a trade-off, and you must decide if you want to run the risk of adding a little bit of fat in exchange for more muscle or sacrifice a little bit of muscle for extra hardness. Unless you're exceptionally lean, I'd advise against eating carbs at night. [Editor's note: You can also tame nocturnal catabolism by using a growth-hormone booster before bed instead of a casein-and-whey drink. The GH can blunt cortisol release, help preserve and build more muscle, and also help burn fat.]

The second technique is to eat in the middle of the night. In that case, you face a new factor on top of the hardness-versus-extra-muscle issue, and that's the quality of sleep. If waking up in the middle of the night makes you irritable the following day, don't do it. If

THE LESSON OF MOTHER'S MILK

You might wonder if the advantages of whey and casein protein counteract each other. Nature provides a particularly bright answer. You probably know that mother's milk contains protein that has an exceptional ability to support very fast growth, but did you know that it's a combination of both whey and casein?[5] With the anabolic properties of whey and the anticatabolic action of casein, mother's milk is an example of a nutrient optimized to support growth.

For bodybuilders, the whey-and-casein combination provides the anabolic effect of whey while counteracting its short-lasting action and its lack of anticatabolic properties. Using the combination between real-food meals allows you to be a bit less strict with your meal timing, and that can be an advantage if you work a nine-to-five job or go to school, where it isn't practical to follow a rigid 6× meal frequency.

THE 6× PROGRAM IN PRACTICE

The 6× program provides the very basic nutrients required for good muscle growth. It's just a skeleton. Add your normal supplementation to it.

Meal 1

When you wake up, have a large whey shake. Don't hesitate to take between 40 and 60 grams of protein. The overnight fast allows your digestive tract to absorb that much right away.

Also, pure protein is better than a meal replacement at this time because carbs have been shown to slow protein absorption.[6] You need to trigger the fast, anabolic actions of whey. Thirty minutes after your protein drink, have a regular breakfast rich in both protein (egg whites, milk, etc.) and carbohydrates (cereals and fruit juice, for example).

slightly more, not a lot more.) Another advantage of frequent eating is that it allows you to control your appetite better. On the downside, however, the smaller meals can be frustrating, which might push you to eat something extra. That quickly translates into fat gains, so you may be better off choosing a casein-and-whey meal-replacement powder instead of whole foods at some feedings. That way, you eat the quantity you planned to eat. Such meals also offer good-quality proteins with no extra calories.

Meal 2

You can have your next meal as much as three hours later. The digestion of whole foods is much slower—and more difficult—than the absorption of protein powders, which is the reason you can wait three hours after breakfast to eat again.

For this meal, high-quality casein protein—in the form of a shake or one or two protein bars—or a whey-and-casein mix is perfect. Depending on your size, try to get between 20 and 40 grams of protein. Carbs are usually included in protein bars. If you go with the shake, you can have a piece of fruit—not because fruit is so great, but rather because it's easy to eat, which makes it convenient for work or school.

Meal 3

Two to three hours later, have a regular meal rich in protein and carbs. Eat some meat along with some vegetable protein. Don't take in more than 40 grams of protein, however, as the proteins from whole foods are harder to digest than powder. You don't want to tax your digestive tract at this point. Favor the carb intake. You'll need it to train hard.

Meal 4

Due to the slow absorption of protein from whole foods, you should space out Meals 3 and 4 so that they're at least three hours apart. Meal 4 is the preworkout feeding, and it should be rich in slow, anticatabolic casein or a whey-and-casein combination plus some carbs. A quality meal replacement will work nicely here. If you cannot train as hard as you want because of this meal, reduce it—say, by using half of a meal-replacement packet. You want the meal to help boost your training intensity, not reduce it.

Workout

I recommend a carb drink during the workout.

Meal 5

Along with breakfast, the postworkout feeding is the most important meal of the day. Intense exercise acts on the 4E-BP1 to make it trap the free eIF4E.[7] That means anabolism is greatly reduced during training. Thanks to the casein you take in before your workout, catabolism will be slowed somewhat but not enough. Once your workout is over, you want to free the eIF4E as fast and as thoroughly as possible. Go for a megadose of whey, taking in 40 to 60 grams of protein. While your body doesn't usually use all of the amino acids, they won't be wasted. They'll be incorporated into albumin, which is a way the body stocks extra proteins for later use.

Thirty minutes after the protein shake, have a normal meal that's rich in protein and moderate in carbs. As with the morning meal, I count the drink and food as one meal.

Meal 6

Just before bed, have a large carb-free whey-and-casein shake, including 30 to 50 grams of protein, for nighttime protection. If you know you're not going to wake up in the middle of the night, you may prefer straight casein. (Note: If you're using a GH booster, which requires an empty stomach, incorporate this drink into Meal 3.) You can also have another carb-free whey-and-casein or straight casein shake in the middle of the night for extra protection if you wish.

References

1. V. N. Litvinova, "Vliianie kratnosti pitaniia na obmen belkov v skeletnykh myshtskh i pecheni belykh krys," *Vopr Pitan* 4: 36 (1976).

2. E. Swanberg, "Amino Acids May Be Intrinsic Regulators of Protein Synthesis in Response to Feeding," *Clinical Nutrition* 17: 77 (1998).

3. C. Jousse, "Physiological Concentration of Amino Acids Regulates Insulinlike-Growth-Factor-Binding Protein 1 Expression," *Biochemistry Journal* 334: 147 (1998).

4. B. R. Britt, "More Frequent Food Intake May Increase Total Energy Intake But Not Body Mass Index," *Faseb J.* 12: A530 (1998).

5. V. Vigi, "Milk Formulae for Normal Infant. II. Recommendations, Energy, Physical Characteristics, and Protein Composition," *Acta Paediat.* 402 (Supplement): 18 (1994).

6. C. Gaudichon, "Acute Interaction of Sucrose or Fat on the Post-Prandial [15N]Labeled Milk Protein Utilization in Humans," *Faseb J.* 12: A860 (1998).

7. L. S. Jefferson, "Availability of eIF4E Regulates Skeletal Muscle Protein Synthesis During Recovery From Training," *American Journal of Physiology* 274: C406 (1998).

INDEX